947   cop. 1

HOFF
Russia

RUSSIA
Adventures in Eyewitness History

RUSSIA

Adventures in Eyewitness History

RHODA HOFF

New York   *HENRY Z. WALCK, Inc.*   *1964*

With this book the author pays tribute to
Barnard College on the occasion of its
Seventy-fifth Anniversary.

LIBRARY OF CONGRESS CATALOG CARD NUMBER: 64–23229
PRINTED IN THE UNITED STATES OF AMERICA

Acknowledgments

Grateful acknowledgment is made to the publishers who kindly gave permission to adapt and use the following material:

"An Exile's Lament." From *The Fasti, Tristia and Pontic Epistles,* by Ovid. Translated by Henry T. Riley. G. Bell & Sons, Ltd., 1903.

"Testament." From *The Russian Primary Chronicle,* by Vladimir Monomakh. Translated by Samuel Cross. Harvard University Press, 1930.

"The Slaves of Russia," by William Richardson. Reprinted from *Seven Britons in Imperial Russia,* edited by Peter Putnam, by permission of Princeton University Press. Copyright 1952 by Princeton University Press.

"The Burning of Moscow." From *With Napoleon in Russia,* by General de Caulaincourt, copyright 1935 by William Morrow and Company, Inc., by permission of William Morrow & Co., Inc., and Librairie Plon.

"A Visit to a Kalmuck Prince." Copyright of translation 1960, 1961 by Alma Elizabeth Murch, translated from the French "En Russie" by Alexandre Dumas. Permission to quote

v

from American edition, *Adventures in Czarist Russia,* granted by Chilton Books, Phila. & N.Y., British edition, Peter Owen Ltd., London.

"The Circle of Tchaykóvsky." From *Memoirs of a Revolutionist,* by P. Kropotkin. Houghton Mifflin Company, 1899.

"Our Life in Kara Prison." From the book *Sixteen Years in Siberia,* by Leo Deutsch. Published by E. P. Dutton & Co., Inc., and reprinted with their permission. Also by permission of John Murray Ltd.

"The Moscow Rising." From *Dawn in Russia,* by Henry W. Nevinson. Harper & Row, 1906.

"The First Duma." From the book *A Year in Russia,* by Maurice Baring. Published by E. P. Dutton & Co., Inc. and reprinted with their permission. Also by permission of the Literary Executor and Methuen & Co. Ltd.

"The Age of Wood." From *Undiscovered Russia,* by Stephen Graham. The Bodley Head Ltd., 1913.

"Lenin's Method of Work." From *Memoirs of Lenin,* by Nadezhda Krupskaya. By permission of International Publishers Co., Inc.

"The Night of the Sixteenth December." From *The End of Rasputin,* by Prince Felix Youssoupoff. Copyright © 1927, 1954 by Prince Felix Youssoupoff. Reprinted by permission of the publishers, The Dial Press, Inc., and Jonathan Cape Ltd.

"Days That Ended the Russian Monarchy." From *The Catastrophe,* by Alexander Kerensky, by permission of Appleton-Century.

Contents

447 B.C.   THE SCYTHIANS   *page 1*
by Herodotus

A.D. 10–15   AN EXILE'S LAMENT   *page 5*
by Ovid

1125   TESTAMENT   *page 8*
by Vladimir Monomakh

1243   THE TARTARS   *page 10*
By Yvo de Narbonne

Early   THE GREAT DUKE OF MOSCOVIA
1500s   AND HIS ARMY   *page 12*
by Sigmund von Herberstein

1551   A LETTER TO THE COUNCIL OF STOGLAV   *page 15*
by Ivan IV, Tsar of Russia

1557   A DINNER WITH TSAR
IVAN THE TERRIBLE   *page 19*
by an Anonymous Eye-Witness

1590   OF THE EMPEROR'S DOMESTIC OR
PRIVATE BEHAVIOUR   *page 21*
by Giles Fletcher

1660s   THE PRIVATE LIFE OF THE BOYARS   *page 24*
by Grigóri Kotoshikhin

1671   STENKO RAZIN,
THE GREAT COSSACK LEADER   *page 28*
by an Anonymous Authority

vii

1685   FROM ASTRAKHAN TO MOSCOW   *page 33*
by Father Avril, S.J.

1701   TRAVELS INTO MUSCOVY   *page 37*
by Cornelis de Bruyn

1701   PETER THE GREAT MAKES SOME REFORMS   *page 42*
by Captain John Perry

1710   THE TSAR PETER THE GREAT   *page 45*
by Charles Lord Witworth

1762   THE JUNE REVOLUTION   *page 47*
by the Princess Daschkaw

1767–   THE SLAVES OF RUSSIA   *page 52*
1769   by William Richardson

1771   ADVENTURES OF A COSSACK SLAVE
IN TARTARY   *page 54*
by Michaelow

1780s   ON RUSSIAN WOMEN   *page 59*
Anonymous

1786   A JOURNEY THROUGH THE CRIMEA   *page 62*
by Elizabeth, Lady Craven

1788   THE RUSSIAN VILLAGE   *page 69*
by Chantreau

1789   THE BARSCHKIRES   *page 73*
by Chantreau

1799   A PARTY: SIBERIAN STYLE   *page 77*
by Augustus von Kotzebue

1800   AN ENCOUNTER WITH SOME TARTARS   *page 80*
by Augustus von Kotzebue

1805   A LETTER FROM ELEANOR CAVANAGH
TO HER FATHER   *page 83*
by Eleanor Cavanagh

1812   THE BATTLE OF BORODINO   *page 88*
by Count Paul Grabbé

1812   THE BURNING OF MOSCOW   *page 92*
by General de Caulaincourt, Duke of Vicenza

1812   LETTER TO ALEXANDER I, TSAR OF RUSSIA   *page 95*
by Napoleon I, Emperor of France

1812–   RUSSIA AND THE WAR WITH NAPOLEON   *page 97*
1813   by John Quincy Adams

1837–   AT THE COURT OF THE TSAR   *page 102*
1838   by George Mifflin Dallas

1840s   THE HUNT   *page 106*
        by Leo N. Tolstoy

1844   THE SECRET POLICE   *page 109*
        by Charles Frederick Henningsen

1852   A LETTER TO MADAME VIARDOT   *page 113*
        by Ivan Turgenev

1854   THE CHARGE OF THE LIGHT BRIGADE   *page 116*
        by General Sir Evelyn Wood, V.C.

1858   A VISIT TO A KALMUCK PRINCE   *page 119*
        by Alexandre Dumas

1861   THE SERF'S MIND   *page 123*
        by an Anonymous Englishman

1865   A RUSSIAN HOME   *page 127*
        by Theophile Gautier

1867   WE ARE RECEIVED BY THE EMPEROR
        OF RUSSIA   *page 130*
        by Mark Twain

1872–   THE CIRCLE OF TCHAYKÓVSKY   *page 133*
1874   by P. Kropotkin

1876   A LETTER TO FLAUBERT   *page 138*
        by Turgenev

1878   OUR LIFE IN KARA PRISON   *page 140*
        by Leo Deutsch

1880–   THE NIHILISTS   *page 144*
1881   by the Dowager Marchioness of Dufferin and Ava

1886   A COURT BALL   *page 148*
        by Mrs. George Van Ness Lothrop

1890   DEPORTATION BY ÉTAPE   *page 151*
        by George Kennan

1892   A FAMINE-STRICKEN VILLAGE   *page 155*
        by Paul von Birukoff

1900s   ON LEO TOLSTOY   *page 160*
        by Maxim Gorky

ix

1904   SIBERIA *page 163*
     by Jules Legras

1904   THE WAR BETWEEN RUSSIA AND JAPAN *page 167*
     by Count Leo Tolstoy

1905   THE MOSCOW RISING *page 172*
     by Henry W. Nevinson

1906   THE FIRST DUMA *page 176*
     by Maurice Baring

1906   ODESSA *page 179*
     by Harry de Windt

1911   THE AGE OF WOOD *page 182*
     by Stephen Graham

1900s   LENIN ON THE PLATFORM *page 186*
     by Leon Trotsky

1900s   LENIN'S METHOD OF WORK *page 189*
     by Nadezhda K. Krupskaya

1916   THE NIGHT OF THE
     SIXTEENTH DECEMBER *page 192*
     by Prince Felix Youssoupoff

1917   DAYS THAT ENDED THE
     RUSSIAN MONARCHY *page 196*
     by Alexander F. Kerensky

1917   THE PEOPLE'S REVOLUTION *page 200*
     by John Reed

Preface

THE WORD "Russia" was first used during the ninth to thirteenth centuries to describe a loose confederation of East Slav tribes centered around the town of Kiev and ruled by princes of the house of Rurik. Before that time, Russian history tells of isolated settlers, some living in the primeval forests of the North, some inhabiting the vast steppe lands to the South. Today Russia is inhabited by some one hundred and seventy different peoples who speak more than two hundred different languages and occupy more than a seventh of all the land on earth. As an old proverb says: "Russia is not a country, but rather a world."

The collection of reports that make up this book does not set out to tell the history of this "world." Rather, it is a series of soundings taken over a period of roughly two thousand years among men and women who have lived, worked, ruled, fought or simply visited in Russia. The first report, written in 447 B.C. by the Greek historian, Herodotus, tells of the strange customs of Scythian tribesmen; in the last account John Reed, an American writer and journalist, describes the "Peoples' Revolution" of 1917. Between these two are men and women from different centuries, different countries and different walks of life.

Different as all these witnesses are, they have one thing in common: each of them has been allowed to speak his mind with a minimum of editorial interference. A few orthographic changes have been made in the interest of readability; now and again, in deference to a shortage of space, cuts have been made. But in no instance has anything been deleted that could obscure a fact of falsify a point of view.

And finally a word of warning. The men and women who report on Russia in this book are all eyewitnesses. That means they are telling of something that they themselves have seen and heard and experienced. This is a vivid, exciting and rewarding branch of history but it is not always an entirely accurate one. For no matter how truthful a witness may be, his eyes may deceive him or his ears may play him false. And in any case, the eyewitness is an integral part of the picture he is describing and therefore cannot see all of it in just perspective. But eyewitness history comes to us "live." It has a warmth and an immediacy that the historian's history can never achieve.

Some of the reports will seem too short to the interested reader; it is hoped that he will turn back to the original book from which the excerpt has been taken. This book offers a sampling of the sights to be seen on a tour of Russia's past. It is then up to each traveler to continue his journey along the route that best fits his particular tastes and his individual needs.

RUSSIA
Adventures in Eyewitness History

447 B.C.

THE SCYTHIANS
by Herodotus

HERODOTUS (485–425 B.C.), one of the greatest historians of all time, was a firm believer in the eyewitness approach to history. In his early twenties he started off on a series of journeys that lasted seventeen years and took him to Greece, the Middle East, North Africa and what is now southern Russia. During these travels he collected much of the material on which he later based his famous history.

Scythia was situated in southern Russia between the Caucasus Mountains and the Danube River. The Romans called the whole region Sarmatia and used the name Scythia only for the country that lay south of the Danube delta which we today know as Dobruga. When Herodotus visited them, the Scythians were a wild nomad tribe whose savage customs the civilized Herodotus confessed he "did not always admire." But he was an objective historian and he was quick to see the tactical advantages that accrue to a people who have neither cities nor forts and who, like snails, carry their dwellings on their backs.

The Scythians have in one respect, and that the most important of all those that fall under man's control, shown themselves wiser than any

1

nation upon the face of the earth. Their customs otherwise are not such as I admire. The one thing of which I speak, is the contrivance whereby they make it impossible for the enemy who invades them to escape destruction, while they themselves are entirely out of his reach, unless it please them to engage with him. Having neither cities, nor forts, and carrying their dwellings with them wherever they go; accustomed, moreover, one and all of them, to shoot from horseback; and living not by husbandry but on their cattle, their wagons the only houses that they possess, how can they fail of being unconquerable, and unassailable even?

The nature of their country, and the rivers by which it is intersected, greatly favour this mode of resisting attacks. For the land is level, well watered and abounding in pastures; while the rivers which traverse it are almost equal in number to the canals of Egypt.

The Scythian soldier drinks the blood of the first man he overthrows in battle. Whatever number he slays, he cuts off all their heads, and carries them to the king; he forfeits all claim if he does not produce a head. The Scyth is proud of these scalps, and hangs them from his bridle-rein; the greater the number that a man can show, the more highly he is esteemed among them. Many make themselves cloaks like the capotes of our peasants, by sewing a quantity of these scalps together. Some even flay the entire body of their enemy, and stretching it upon a frame, carry it about with them wherever they ride. Such are the Scythian customs with respect to scalps and skins.

Once a year the governor of each district, at a set place in his own province, mingles a bowl of wine, of which all the Scythians have a right to drink by whom foes have been slain; while they who have slain no enemy are not allowed to taste of the bowl, but sit aloof in disgrace. No greater shame than this can happen to them. Such as have slain a very large number of foes, have two cups instead of one, and drink from both.

Scythia has an abundance of soothsayers, who foretell the future by means of willow wands. A large bundle of these wands is brought and laid on the ground. The soothsayer unties the bundle, and places each wand by itself, at the same time uttering his prophecy: then, while he is still speaking, he gathers the rods together again, and makes them up once more into a bundle. This mode of divination is of home growth in Scythia.

Whenever the Scythian king falls sick, he sends for the three soothsayers of most renown at the time, who come and make trial of their art in the mode above described. Generally they say that the king is ill, because such or such a person, mentioning his name, has sworn falsely by the royal hearth. This is the usual oath among the Scythians. Then the man accused of having forsworn himself is arrested and brought before the king. The soothsayers tell him that by their art it is clear he has sworn a false oath by the royal hearth, and so caused the illness of the king—he denies the charge, protests that he has sworn no false oath, and loudly complains of the wrong done to him. Upon this the king sends for six new soothsayers, who try the matter by soothsaying. If they too find the man guilty of the offense, straightway he is beheaded by those who first accused him, and his goods are parted amongst them: if, on the contrary, they acquit him, other soothsayers, and again others, are sent for to try the case. Should the greater number decide in favour of a man's innocence, then they who first accused him forfeit their lives.

Oaths among the Scythians are accompanied with the following ceremonies: a large earthen bowl is filled with wine, and the parties to the oath, wounding themselves slightly with a knife or an awl, drop some of their blood into the wine; then they plunge into the mixture a scymitar, some arrows, a battle-ax, and a javelin, all the while repeating prayers; lastly the two contracting parties drink each a draught from the bowl, as do also the chief men among their followers.

3

What the population of Scythia is, I was not able to learn with certainty. I heard from some that they were very numerous indeed; others made their numbers but scanty for such a nation as the Scyth. Thus much, however, I witnessed with my own eyes. There is a tract called Exampaeus between the Borysthenes [the Dnieper] and the Hypanis [an arm of the Dnieper]. Here stands a brazen bowl, six times as big as that at the entrance of the Euxine [the Black Sea]. Such as have never seen that vessel may understand me better if I say that the Scythian bowl holds with ease six hundred amphorae [over 5,000 gallons] and is of the thickness of six fingers breadth. The natives gave me the following account of the manner in which it was made. One of their kings, by name Ariantas, wishing to know the number of his subjects, ordered them all to bring him, on pain of death, the point off one of their arrows. They obeyed; and he collected thereby a vast heap of arrow-heads, which he resolved to form into a memorial that might go down to posterity. Accordingly he made of them this bowl, and dedicated it at Exampaeus. This was all that I could learn concerning the number of the Scythians.

The country has no marvels except its rivers, which are larger and more numerous than those of any other land. These, and the vastness of the great plain, are worthy of note. And one thing besides. They show a footmark of Hercules, impressed on a rock, in shape like the print of a man's foot, but two cubits in length.

AN EXILE'S LAMENT
by Ovid

Publius Ovidius Naso, who became famous as the poet Ovid, was born on the 20th of March, 43 B.C., in a small town in the Appenines about ninety miles from Rome.

He went to Rome to study law and rhetoric; but, feeling himself unsuited to these pursuits, he determined to be a poet against the advice of his father, who pointed out to him that even the great poet Homer had died a poor man. In spite of this dire prophecy, Ovid soon made a name for himself, married three times, and lived a pleasant existence until he was fifty-one when he was banished from Rome by the edict of the Emperor Augustus. The cause of his banishment is not known, although it is thought that the reason was probably a political one.

The place of his exile was Tomi, a Roman colony on the Black Sea. Tomi was on the very frontier of civilization; the climate was bleak, and the inhabitants led a rude and primitive existence. Ovid was miserably unhappy at Tomi; but, although he made repeated applications both to Augustus and his successor, Tiberius, for a remission of his sentence, his pleas were ignored. He died in exile at the age of fifty-nine.

If any one, yonder, remembers the banished Naso, let him know that I am living in the midst of barbarism, exposed under stars that never set in the ocean. The Sauromatae, a savage race, the Bessi and the Getae surround me. Yet, while the air is mild, we are defended by the intervening Danube; while it flows, it repels invasion by its waves. But when dire winter has put forth his rugged face, and the earth has become white with ice, hard as marble; when Boreas is at liberty, and snow has been sent upon the regions under the Bear; then it is true that these nations are distressed by a shivering climate. The snow lies *deep;* and as it lies, neither sun nor rain melts it;

Boreas hardens it, and makes it endure for ever; hence, when the former ice has not yet melted, fresh succeeds, and in many a place it is wont to last for two years.

So great is the strength of the North wind, when aroused, that it levels high towers with the ground, and carries off roofs borne away: the inhabitants poorly defend themselves from the cold by skins and sewn trousers; and of the whole body, the face is the only part exposed. Often, the hair, as it is moved, rattles with the pendent icicle, and the white beard shines with the ice that has formed upon it. Liquid wine becomes solid, preserving the form of the vessel: they do not quaff draughts of liquor, but pieces which are presented.

The Danube itself, which, no narrower than the river that bears the papyrus, mingles, through many mouths, with the vast ocean, freezes as the winds harden its azure streams, and it rolls to the sea with covered waters; where ships had gone, they now walk on foot; and the hoof of the horse strikes the waters hardened by freezing. Sarmatian oxen drag the uncouth wagons along unwonted bridges, as the waters roll beneath; indeed, I shall scarcely be believed; but inasmuch as there is no profit in untruths, an eye-witness ought to receive full confidence. I have seen the vast sea frozen with ice, and a slippery crust covered the unmoved waters. I have trod upon the hardened ocean, and the surface of the water was under my foot, not wetted by it. The ships stand, hemmed in by the frost, as though by marble, and no oar can cleave the stiffened water.

I have seen fish remain bound fast in ice, and even then some part of them retained life; immediately, the Danube being made level by the drying Northern blasts, the barbarous enemy is carried over on his swift steed: an enemy strong in horses, and in the arrow that flies from afar, depopulates the neighbouring region far and wide. Some take to flight, and no one being left to protect the fields, the unguarded property becomes a prey; such as cattle, and the creaking wagons, the little treasures of the country, and the riches besides that the poor inhabitant possesses; some are driven along as captives, with their arms fastened behind their backs, looking back in vain upon their fields and their homes; some die in torments, pierced by barbed arrows, for on the winged steel there is a poison, in which it has been dipped. What they cannot carry with themselves, or lead away, they destroy, and the flames of the enemy consume the unoffending cottages; even when there is peace, they cause alarm from the apprehension of war, and no one ploughs the ground with the pressed ploughshare.

This spot either beholds the enemy, or is always in dread of a foe; the earth deserted, becomes worthless, left untilled in ruinous neglect. You may behold naked plains without trees—without leaves; places, alas! not to be visited by a fortunate man!

If I look at the place, it is odious. If I look at the men: the men are hardly worthy of that name, and they have more savage ferocity than wolves. They regard not laws, but right yields to might, and justice, overcome, lies prostrate under the warlike sword. They poorly repel the cold, with skins and flowing trousers; and their faces are rough, covered with long hair.

Innumerable tribes around are threatening cruel warfare; tribes which deem it a disgrace not to live by rapine. Outside, nothing is safe; the hill is but poorly defended by small fortifications. When you would least expect it, the enemy, in a dense mass, like birds, is flying down upon you, and, before he is well seen, is driving off his prey. Often do we pick up in the midst of the streets their dangerous arrows, that have come within the fortifications, when the gates have been shut. There are few, therefore, that dare to live out in the country; and they, wretched people, plough with one hand, and hold their arms with the other. Covered with a helmet, the shepherd plays on his oaten pipe, joined with pitch. Here it is I who am the bar-

barian, because by no one am I understood; the stupid Getae laugh at Latin words.

I lament, my friends, both that I am deprived of the light of my country and of yourselves, and that I am here in the Scythian land.

1125

TESTAMENT
by Vladimir Monomakh

VLADIMIR MONOMAKH, Grand Prince of Kiev (1053–1125), was the son of Yaroslav the Wise, who was also a Grand Prince of Kiev, and of the Byzantine Emperor Constantine's daughter. In a rough and turbulent age, he was a strong ruler, an honorable man, a great hunter and a pious son of the church. He believed in "living dangerously" and in trusting God, ideals which he transmitted to his sons.

In 1103, before he had been made Grand Prince, Vladimir Monomakh led a united Russian army deep into the steppes, winning a victory that ended the civil wars which had been raging in Russia for more than ten years.

The excerpt that follows is Monomakh's last will and testament. But although he was already ill, or, as he puts it, "about to seat myself in the sleigh" [in Russia in ancient times the dead were always taken away in sleighs], he writes with vigor and fervor. The testament is interesting both as a portrait of a man of the twelfth century and as a picture of life in a rude age.

I now narrate to you, my sons, the fatigue I have endured in journeys and hunts for fifty-three years.

Among all my campaigns, there are eighty-three long ones, and I do not count the minor adventures.

I concluded nineteen peace treaties with the Polovcians with or without my father's aid, and dispensed much of my cattle and my

8

garments. I freed from their captivity the best Polovcian princes, including two brothers of Sharukan, three brothers of Bagubars, and one hundred of their foremost leaders. Of other chieftains whom God delivered alive into my hands, I took captive, killed and had cast into the river Slavyla Koxus and his son, Aklan, Burchivich, Azgului prince of Tarev, and fifteen other young chieftains, and at the same time not less than two hundred of the leading prisoners were killed, and cast into the same river.

I devoted much energy to hunting as long as I reigned in Chernigov and made excursions from that city. Until the present year, in fact, I without difficulty used all my strength in hunting, not to mention other hunting expeditions around Turov, since I had been accustomed to chase every sort of game while in my father's company.

At Chernigov, I even bound wild horses with my bare hands or captured ten or twenty live horses with the lasso, and besides that, while riding along the Rus, I caught those same wild horses bare handed. Two bisons tossed me and my horse on their horns, a stag once gored me, one elk stamped upon me, while another gored me, a boar once tore my sword from my thigh, a bear on one occasion bit my kneecap; and another wild beast jumped on my flank and threw my horse with me. But God preserved me unharmed.

I often fell from my horse, fractured my skull twice, and in my youth injured my arms and legs when I did not reck of my life or spare my head. In war and at the hunt, by night and by day, in heat and cold, I did whatever my servant had to do, and gave myself no rest. Without relying on lieutenants or messengers, I did whatever was necessary; I looked to every disposition in my household. At the hunt, I posted the hunters, and I looked after the stable, the falcons and the hawks. I did not allow the mighty to distress the common peasant or the poverty-stricken widow, and interested myself in the church administration and service.

Let not my sons or whoever else reads this document criticise me. I do not commend my own boldness, but I praise God and glorify his memory because he guarded me, a sinful and a wretched man, for so many years in these dangerous vicissitudes, and did not make me inactive or useless for all the necessary work of man. As you read this screed prepare yourselves for all good works, and glorify God among his saints. Without fear of death, of war, or of wild beasts, do a man's work, my sons, as God sets it before you. If I suffered no ill from war, from wild beasts, from flood or from falling from my horse, then surely no one can harm and destroy you, unless that too be destined of God. But if death comes from God, then neither father, nor mother, nor brethren can hinder it, and though it is prudent to be constantly on one's guard, the protection of God is fairer than the protection of man.

1243

THE TARTARS
by Yvo de Narbonne

In the thirteenth century the Tartars came out of the east to invade and conquer Russia. In a letter to the Archbishop of Bordeaux, Yvo de Narbonne, a young French knight who had gone to fight this Moslem army in the name of Christendom, gives the earliest eyewitness account of the Tartars that has been preserved.

The Tartars are covetous, irascible, deceitful, and merciless, beyond all men; yet through the rigour of discipline which is exercised by their superiors, they are restrained from brawls and murderous strife. They esteem the ancient founders and fathers of their tribes as Gods, in whose honour they celebrate solemn feasts at certain fixed times; and these deities are very numerous, though only four are considered as general gods of the nation. They consider all things as created for their sole use, and do not therefore think themselves cruel or unjust in wasting and destroying the surrounding nations, whom they esteem rebels against their legitimate authority. Their bodies, though lean, are hardy and strong, with broad chests and square high shoulders, strong well knit joints and firm sinews, thick and large thighs, with short legs, so that being equal to us in stature, what they want in their legs is supplied in the upper part of their bodies. Their faces are pale, with short flat noses, their eyes black and inconstant, having large eyebrows, extending down to the nose; long sharp chins, their upper jaws low and declining, their teeth long and their countenances distorted, fierce and terrible.

In ancient times their country, which is situated far beyond Chaldea, was utterly waste and barren, from whence they have expelled the lions, bears, and other wild beasts. Of the tanned hides of beasts they make themselves light but impenetrable armour, and their backs are only slightly armed, that they may not flee in battle. They use small but strong horses, which are maintained with little provender. In fight they use javelins, maces, battle-axes, and swords, but are particularly expert in the use of bows and arrows. When engaged in battle they never retire till they see the chief standard of their general give back. When vanquished they ask no quarter and in victory they show no compassion; and though many millions in number, they all persist as one man, in resolving to subdue the whole world under their dominion. They have 60,000 couriers who are sent before on light horses to prepare a place for the army to encamp, and these will gallop in one night as far as our troops can march in three days. When they invade a country, they suddenly diffuse themselves over the whole land, surprising the people unarmed, unprovided, and dispersed, and make such horrible slaughter and devastation, that the king and prince of the invaded land cannot collect a sufficient force to give them battle.

Sometimes they say, they intend to go to Cologne to bring home the three wise kings into their own country; sometimes they propose to punish the avarice and pride of the Romans, who formerly oppressed them; sometimes to conquer the barbarous nations of the north; sometimes to moderate the fury of the Germans with their own mildness; sometimes in derision they say that they intend going on a pilgrimage to the shrine of St. James in Galicia. By means of these pretenses, some indiscreet governors of provinces have entered into league with them, and have granted them free passage through their territories; but which leagues they have ever violated, to the certain ruin and destruction of these princes and their unhappy countries.

Early 1500s

THE GREAT DUKE OF MOSCOVIA AND HIS ARMY
by Sigmund von Herberstein

SIGMUND, FREIHERR VON HERBERSTEIN, was an Austrian diplomat, student of history and experienced traveler. He was one of the earliest foreign observers to give an account of Russia, and his report was so perceptive and so objective that today he is still accounted an authority by Russian historians.

Of the princes that now reign in Russia, the chief is the great Duke of Moscovia who possesseth the greatest part thereof.

In authority and dominion over his subjects, the prince of Moscovia passeth all the monarchs of the world. For he depriveth all his noble men and gentlemen of all their holdings and munitions at his pleasure. He trusteth not his own brothers, but oppresseth all with like servitude. In so much that whomsoever he commandeth either to remain with him in court, or to go to the wars, or sendeth on ambassage, they are compelled to be at their own charge, except the young gentlemen, the sons of the Boiarons [Boyars], that is, the noble men of the lowest degree. He usurpeth this authority as well over the spiritual as over the temporal: constituting what him listeth of the goods and life of all men. Of his counselors there is not one that dare dissent from him in any thing. They openly confess that the will of the prince is the will of god, and believe him to be the executor of god's will. By reason whereof, the prince himself when any petition is made to him for the delivery of any captive, is accustomed to answer thus: God knoweth and the great prince. It is uncertain whether the cruelty and fierceness of the nation do require so tyranous a prince, or whether by the tyranny of the prince, the nation is made so fierce and cruel.

The prince every second or third year, causeth a muster to be taken of the sons of the Boiarons, and taketh an account both of their number and how many horse and men every one of them is able to give: and then appointeth a certain stipend of such as are able to bear their own charges in the wars. They have seldom any rest or quietness. For they either keep war with the Lithuanians, Livinians, Suetians, or Tartars. Or if it so chance that the prince keepeth no war, yet doth he yearly appoint garrisons of thousands of men in places about Tanaris and Occa to repress the incursions and robberies of the European Tartars.

The Muscovites in placing their army, choose a large plain where the best of them pitch their tent and others make arbours of bows fixt in the ground, bending together the tops thereof, which they cover with their cloaks to defend themselves, their bows, arrows, saddles and other necessaries from rain.

It may perhaps seem strange how he maintaineth him and his so long with so small an army as I have said. I will now therefore briefly declare their sparing and frugality. He who has five or more horses, giveth one of them as a pack horse to bear all necessaries. He hath also in a bag of two or three spans long, the flour or meal of the grain called millet: and VIII or X pounds weight of swines' flesh powdered. He hath likewise a bag of salt, mixed with pepper if he be rich. Furthermore every man carrieth with him a hatchet, a fire-pot, and a brazen pot: so that if they chance to come to any place where they can find no fruits, garlick, onions or flesh, they kindle a fire and fill their pots with water whereunto they put a spoonful of meal with a quantity of salt, and make pottage thereof, wherewith the master and all his servants live contented. But if the master be very hungry, he eateth all alone, and the servants are sometimes forced to fast for the space of two or three days. And if the master intend to fare somewhat more delicately, then he addeth thereto a little portion of swine's flesh. I speak not thus of the best of them, but of such as are the mean sort. The governors and captains of the army, do sometimes bid the poorer sort to their tables: where they feed themselves so well, that they fast two or three days after. When they have fruits, garlick, and onions, they can well forbear all other meats. Proceeding forward to the battle, they put more confidence in their multitude, and with what great armies they assail their enemies, than in the strength and valour of their soldiers, or in well instructing their army: and fight better afar off, than at hand: and therefore study how to circumvent or enclose their enemies and to assail them on the back half.

They have many trumpeters: the which while they blow all at once after their manner, make a marvelous strange noise. They have also another kind of instrument which they call Szurna. These may blow without ceasing for the space of an hour together, so tempering the same and holding in the wind which they draw more, that the noise seemeth continued without intermission.

They wear all one manner of apparel: as long coats without pleats and with narrow sleeves after the manner of the Hungarians. These and Christians use to button on the right side: and the Tartars (using the like) button them on the left side. They wear red and short buskins that reach not to their knees; and have the soles thereof defended with plates of iron. In manner all their shirts are wrought with divers colours about the neck: and have the collars and ruffs beset with little round balls like beads, of silver or gilded copper, and sometimes pearls also.

1551

A LETTER TO THE COUNCIL OF STOGLAV
by Ivan IV, Tsar of Russia

IN 1551, the high dignitaries of the Russian Church met in the Kremlin at Moscow at the order of Tsar Ivan IV to discuss the general reform of the church.

Ivan had succeeded to the throne as a very young child. The first years of his reign passed peacefully enough under the rule of his mother; but when the boy was only eight years old she was poisoned, and a group of boyars took control of the country. At public gatherings they treated the young Ivan with respect, but the rest of the time the boy lived virtually as a prisoner, isolated from his relatives, neglected and uneducated except for such scraps of knowledge as he could forage for himself from reading books. But Ivan was a strong and gifted boy, and when he was only thirteen, he sent for his boyars, denounced them, arrested some, and had others put to death.

Having shown his power, he invited his mother's relatives to rule for him until he should feel able to take over the reigns of government himself, which he did in due course, becoming one of Russia's strongest tsars.

From the time he was a boy he had read the scriptures, and under the influence of a religious wife his interest in the church deepened. The Council of Stoglav coincided with the height of his religious period.

But Ivan had another side to his nature. Although he made many reforms, he was a man of violent passions. He struck his own son a blow that killed him, and the brutality with which he enforced his reforms earned him the name of "the Terrible." He alternated all his life long between states of wild passion and equally wild penitence; the letter he sent to the Council of Stoglav shows him in one of his repentant moods.

Recently, because various sins have been committed, many cities have been ruined, men have disappeared never to return again, and great regions have been devastated. Some men have sinned through pride, others through hatred of their brothers, and still others because they have done violence to their own people. Many who have worshipped idols have perished.

Let us be fearful of the same fate. Let us purify the aspirations of our souls, let us put behind us the transient phantoms that have momentarily blinded our eyes, let us see if we have not been infected by those very evils of which I have been speakng. You may tell me that we are not idol worshippers. But if you love money, does that not mean that you are worshipping an idol? You know better than I know myself to what extent I have been the slave of money. You may answer that I have not been guilty of violating the law? But I dare to say with the Prophet, that I am like a snake who remains deaf to the voices of those who seek to charm it. Nevertheless God has been merciful to us; he has punished us in divers ways but even as his benevolence chastised us, it led us from the path of evil as a father does who cherishes his children.

God has taken from me a father and from you a protector and a shepherd. My sorrow has not yet been assuaged: From all sides I have been assailed by great misfortunes, great sorrows. The boyars, the great lords, who in the past were devoted to my ancestors, gave me disastrous counsel: they professed a great enthusiasm for me, but in reality, they thought only of strengthening their own power. They dared to seize my father's brothers and then put them to death. When I think of the cruel end which my uncles met with, the pitiless punishment which they suffered, I weep. I am penitent and I ask them to forgive me my youth and my inexperience.

Only a short while after my uncles died, my mother died too, and I suffered another bitter sorrow. I was an orphan: my kingdom was like a wife who has been bereft of her husband. At this time our boyars decided that the moment had come which would be favorable to their purposes: they governed the kingdom according to their whim, for there was no one to oppose them in the exercise of their fatal power. My sins, my isolation, my youth, were to blame for the fact that many people perished in the horrors attendant on a civil war.

I grew up without the guidance of either a father or a mother, deprived of those lessons which only a tenderly loving father can give to his child. From the men who surrounded me, I learned evil prac-tises until at last I became as deceitful as they were. From that time until to-day, with what sins have I not offended my God! I have watched my people being led off into captivity, I have stood by as churches were devastated, holy objects were trodden underfoot, blood flowed in streams, flames were unleashed, and priests and monks were taken captive. Princes, boyars, christians of both sexes, were scattered over the far corners of the earth, outraged and defiled, and, after all the suffering they had undergone, were delivered over to death.

Many times we have sought to revenge ourselves on our enemies but our efforts have been in vain. We did not understand that our

17

misfortunes were the punishment of God and not the triumph of the heathen. These harsh punishments did not bring us to repentance. Instead we provoked a civil war with all its attendant horrors, and unhappy christians, were the victims of all this violence. Then God, in his infinite mercy, punished our innumerable sins by sending us floods, plagues, and a thousand other ills. Even these lessons were wasted on us: then God sent a terrible conflagration and the patrimony that I had inherited from my ancestors perished in flames [he is alluding to the burning of Moscow in 1547].

At last terror invaded my soul. My heart was humbled and I acknowledged my sins. I sought refuge in the Holy Church: I prostrated myself before God, who is ever filled with loving tenderness for man, I knelt before the Mother of God, before all the saints, before your authority, most reverend fathers. Filled with sincere remorse, I have asked forgiveness for all the evil I have done, and through the inexhaustible grace of God, I have obtained from you, peace, benediction and pardon for all my transgressions.

In fulfillment of your desires, my princes, my boyars, after they had pledged their faith to me, have been pardoned by me for all the sins which they committed against me. Aided by your counsel, I have begun to rule the kingdom which God has confided to me, relying on the support of Providence. I implore God to help me. I beg you also, holy and venerable assembly, to pray for me to the all powerful and all merciful God.

Should I ever resist your unanimous decisions, should I ever violate the divine Law, I beg of you: do not be silent. Should I ever disobey you, I urge you to oppose me without fear, in order that the life of my own soul, and of the souls of my subjects, shall be safeguarded. And so that we may uphold the orthodox Christian Law in all its purity, so that through it the august name of the Father, the Son, and the Holy Ghost shall triumph now, in the years to follow, and in all the centuries to come.

A DINNER WITH TSAR IVAN THE TERRIBLE
by an Anonymous Eye-Witness

"ON THE 12TH MAY in the year of our Lord 1557, there departed from Gravesend four good ships bound into the Bay of St. Nicholas in Russia, in which was transported one Ossep Gregoriwich Napea." Napea had been Russian ambassador to England and he was returning for good to his home country.

On their arrival in Russia the ships' companies were invited to dine with the Tsar, Ivan IV. It was quite a festive occasion and the description of it that follows gives an excellent picture of the munificence of Russian hospitality as seen through sober British eyes.

The 14th of September we were commanded to come unto the Emperor and immediately after our coming we were brought into the presence, unto whom each of us did his duty accordingly and kissed his right hand, his Majesty sitting in his chair of state, with his crown on his head and a staff of goldsmith's work in his left hand well garnished with rich and costly stones; and when we had all kissed his hand and done our duty, his Majesty did declare by his interpreter that we were all welcome unto him, and unto his country, and thereupon willed us to dine with him that day. We gave thanks unto his Majesty, and so departed until the dinner was ready.

When dinner-time approached we were brought again into the Emperor's dining chamber, where we were set on one side of a table that stood over against the Emperor's table, to the end that he might well behold us all.

All the tables were covered only with salt and bread, and after that we had sat awhile, the Emperor sent unto every one of us a piece of bread, which was given and delivered unto every man severally with these words: "The Emperor and Great Duke giveth thee bread this day"; and in like manner three or four times before dinner was ended he sent unto every man drink, which was given with these words: "The Emperor and Great Duke giveth thee to drink." All the tables were served in vessels of pure and fine gold, as well as basins and ewers, platters, dishes and saucers, as also great pots, with an innumerable sort of small drinking pots of divers fashions, whereof a great number were set with stone. As for costly meats, I have many times seen better; but for change of wines and divers sorts of meads, it was wonderful; for there was not left at any time so much void room on the table that one cup more might have been set, and as far as I could perceive all the rest were in like manner served.

In the dinner-time there came in six singers who stood in the midst of the chamber, and their faces towards the Emperor, who sang there before dinner was ended three several times, whose songs or voices delighted our ears little or nothing.

The Emperor never putteth morsel of meat in his mouth but he blesseth it himself, and in like manner as often as he drinketh; for after his manner he is very religious, and he esteemeth his religious persons above his noblemen.

This dinner continued for about the space of five hours, which being ended, and the tables taken up, we came into the midst of the chamber, where we did reverence unto the Emperor's Majesty, and then he delivered unto every one of us with his own hands a cup of mead, which when every man had received and drunk a quantity thereof we were licensed to depart, and so ended the dinner. And because the Emperor would have us be merry, he sent to our lodging the same evening three barrels of mead of sundry sort, of the quantity in all of one hogshead.

The 16th day of September the Emperor sent home into our lodging for every one of us a Tartary horse to ride from place to place as we had occasion, for the streets of Moscow are very foul and miry in summer.

20

The 18th of September there were given unto Master Standish, doctor in physic, and the rest of our men of our occupations, certain furred gowns of branched velvet and gold, and some of red damask, of which Master Doctor's gown was furred with sables, and the rest were furred, some with white ermine, and some with grey squirrel, and all faced and edged round about with black beaver.

1590

OF THE EMPEROR'S DOMESTIC OR PRIVATE BEHAVIOUR
by Giles Fletcher

GILES FLETCHER, Queen Elizabeth I's ambassador to Russia, was an astute and experienced observer. His ambition was to note things that were "rather true than strange." He found the country of the tsars to be a "tyrannical state (most unlike our own) without true knowledge of God, without written Lawe, without common Justice."

The reigning Tsar was Theodore I, the second son of Ivan the Terrible, a stupid, good-natured, pious man who delegated the governing of the country to his brother-in-law, Boris Godunov, while he himself prayed, dined well, and amused himself amiably. Theodore died in 1598 and, as he had no children, the royal house that was descended from Rurik, and that had ruled Russia for seven hundred years, became extinct.

The Emperor's private behaviour so much as may be, or is meete to be known, is after this manner. He riseth about 4 o'clock in the morning. After his apparelling and washing, in cometh his ghostly father, or priest of his chamber, with his cross in his hand, wherewith he blesseth him, laying it first on his forehead, then upon his cheeks, or sides of his face, and then offreth him the end of it to kiss. This done, the Clerk of his cross bringeth unto his chamber, a painted image representing the Saint of that day. For ever day with them hath his several Saint, as it were the patron of that day. This he placeth among the rest of his image gods, wherewith all his chamber is decked, as thick almost as the wall can bear, with lamps and wax candles burning before them. They are very costly and decked with pearls and precious stones. This image being placed before him, the Emperor beginneth to cross himself. Thus he continueth the space of a quarter of an hour or thereabouts. Then cometh again the ghostly father with a silver bowl full of holy water. This holy water is brought fresh every day from the monasteries, far and near, sent to the Emperor from the Abbot or Prior.

These devotions being ended, he sendeth in to the Empress, to ask whether she hath rested in health. And after a little pause, goes himself to salute her. After their meeting they go together to their private church or chapel, where is said, or sung, a morning service. From the church he returneth home, and sitteth him down in a great chamber, to be seen or saluted by his Nobility, such as are in favour about the Court.

About nine in the morning, he goeth to another church within his castle: where is sung by Priests, and Chorister, the high Service, which commonly lasteth two hours: the Emperor in the meantime talking commonly with some of his Council and the Council likewise confer together among themselves, as if they were in their Council house. This ended, he returneth home, and recreateth himself until it be dinnertime.

He is served at his table in this manner. First every dish (as it is delivered at the dresser) is tasted by the Cook, in the presence of the high Steward, or his Deputy. And so is received by the Gentlemen waiters and by them carried up to the Emperor's table, the high

22

Steward or Deputy going before. There it is received by the Server who giveth a taste of every dish to the Taster, and so placeth it before the Emperor. The number of his dishes for his ordinary service is about seventy: dressed somewhat grossly with much garlick, & salt. When he exceedeth upon some occasion of the day, or entertainment of some Ambassador, he hath many more dishes. The service is sent up by two dishes at a time, or three at the most, that he may eat it warm, first the baked, then the roast meats, & last the broths. In his dining chamber is another table: where sit the chief of his Nobility and his ghostly father or Chaplain.

After dinner he layeth him down to rest, where commonly he taketh three hours sleep, except he employ one of his hours to bathing or boxing. And this custom for sleeping after dinner, is an ordinary matter with him, as with all the Russes. After his sleep, he goeth to evensong and thence returning for the most part recreateth himself with the Empress till supper time, with jesters, and dwarfes, men and women, that tumble before him, and sing many songs after the Russe manner. This is his common recreation between meals, that he most delights in.

One other special recreation is the fight with wild Bears, which are caught in pits or nets, and are kept in barred cages for that purpose, against the Emperor be disposed to see the pastime. The fight with the Bear is of this sort. The man is turned into a circle walled round about, where he is to quite himself so well as he can: for there is no way to fly out. When the Bear is turned loose he cometh upon him with open mouth. If at the first push he miss his aim, so that the Bear come within him, he is in great danger. But the wild Bear being very fierce, hath this quality that giveth advantage to the Hunter. His manner is when he assaileth a man, to rise up right on his two hinder legs, and so to come roaring with open mouth upon him. And if the Hunter then can push right into the very breast of him betwixt his forelegs, resting the other end of his boarespear at the side of his foot, & so keeping the pike still towards the face of the Bear, he speedeth him commonly at one blow. But many times these Hunters come short and are either slain or miserably torn with the teeth and talons of the fierce beast. If the party quite himself well in this fight with the Bear, he is carried to drink at the Emperor's cellar door: where he drinketh himself drunk for the honor of *Hospodare*. And this is his reward for adventuring his life, for the Emperor's pleasure.

This is his recreation commonly on the holy days. Sometimes he spendeth his time in looking upon his goldsmith's, and jewellers, tailors, embroiderers, painters, & such like, & so goeth to his supper. When it draweth towards bed time, his priest sayeth certain prayers: and then the Emperor blesseth and crosseth himself, as in the morning for a quarter of an hour or thereabouts, and so goeth to his bed.

The Emperor that now is (called *Theodore Ivanowich*) is for his person of a mean stature, somewhat low and gross, of a sallow complexion, and inclining to the dropsie, hawk-nosed, unsteady in his pace by reason of some weakness of his limbs, heavy and inactive, yet commonly smiling almost to a laughter. For quality otherwise, simple and slow witted, but very gentle, and of an easy nature, quiet, merciful, of no martial disposition, nor greatly apt for matter of policy, very superstitious, and infinite that way. Besides his private devotions at home, he goeth every week commonly on pilgrimage to some Monastery, or other that is nearest hand. He is 34 years old, or thereabouts, and hath reigned almost the space of six years.

1660s

THE PRIVATE LIFE OF THE BOYARS
by Grigóri Kotoshikhin

GRIGÓRI KOTOSHIKHIN was a clerk in the Department of Legations in Moscow. From time to time he was used as an ambassador in connection with various treaties that were being arranged between Russia and Sweden and Poland. In 1664 he was in the field with the Russian army that was fighting Poland when the two generals in charge were recalled. General Dolgoruki was sent out to replace them and he tried to get Kotoshikhin to help him prove that the dismissed generals had been traitors. Kotoshikhin refused and, afraid that the general would be angry with him for his refusal, fled Russia and took refuge in Sweden. He lived in Stockholm for some years working in the Foreign Office in an unofficial capacity, until he got into a drunken brawl with a man and killed him. He was beheaded for this crime in 1667.

During his stay in Sweden, Kotoshikhin wrote a book on Russian customs which is outstanding for its picture of the society of his time.

Boyars and Near People [lowest rank of nobles] live in their houses, both of stone and wood, that are not well arranged; their wives and children live all in separate rooms. Only a few of the greater boyars have their own churches in their courts; and those of the high and middle boyars who have no churches of their own, but who are permitted to have priests at their houses, have the matins and vespers and other prayers said in their own apartments, but they attend mass in any church they may choose; they never have the mass in their own houses. The boyars and Near People pay their priests a yearly salary, according to agreement; if the priests are married people, they receive a monthly allowance of food, but the widowed priests eat at the same table with their boyars.

25

It is their custom to prepare simple dishes, without seasoning, without berries, or sugar, without pepper, ginger or other spices, and they are little salted and without vinegar. They place on the table one dish at a time; the other dishes are brought from the kitchen and are held in the hands by the servants. The dishes that have little vinegar, salt and pepper are seasoned at the table; there are in all fifty to one hundred such dishes.

Before dinner the hosts order their wives to come out and greet their guests. When the women come, they place themselves in the hall, or room, where the guests are dining, at the place of honour, and the guests stand at the door; the women greet the guests with the small salute, but the guests bow to the ground. Then the host makes a low obeisance to his guests, the host kisses his wife first; then the guests make individual bows and, stepping forward, kiss his wife and, walking back again, bow to her once more; she makes the small salute each time she kisses a guest. Then the hostess brings each guest a glass of brandy, the size of the glass being the fourth of a quart. The host makes as many low obeisances as there are guests, asking each one to partake of the brandy his wife is offering them. By the request of the guests, the host bids his wife to drink first, then he drinks himself, and then the guests are served.

After this drinking the hostess makes a bow to the guests and retires to her apartments to meet her guests, the wives of the boyars. The hostess and wives of the guests never dine with the men, except at weddings; an exception is also made when the guests are near relatives and there are no outsiders present at the dinner. During the dinner, the host and guests drink after every course a cup of brandy, or Rhine wine, and spiced and pure beer, and various kinds of mead. When they bring the round cakes to the table, the host's daughters-in-law, or married daughters, or the wives of near relatives come into the room, and the guests rise and, leaving the table, go to the door and salute the women; then the husbands of the women salute them, and beg the guests to kiss their wives and drink the wine they offer. The guests comply with their request and return to the table, while the women go back to their apartments. After dinner the host and guests drink more freely each other's healths, and drive home again. The boyars' wives dine and drink in the same manner in their own apartments, where there are no men present.

The boyars and Near People have in their houses 100, or 200, or 300, or 500, or 1000 servants, male and female, according to their dignity and possessions. These servants receive a yearly salary, if they are married, 2, 3, 5 or 10 roubles, according to their services, and their wearing apparel, and a monthly allowance of bread and victuals; they live in their own rooms in the court of the boyar's house. The best of these married servants are sent out by the boyars every year, by rotation, to their estates and villages, with the order to collect from their peasants the taxes and rents. The unmarried older servants receive some small wages, but the younger ones receive nothing: all the unmarried servants get their wearing apparel, hats, shirts, and boots; the older of these servants live in the farther lower apartments, and receive their food and drink from the kitchen; on holidays they receive two cups of brandy each. The female servants who are widows remain living in the houses of their husbands, and they receive a yearly wage and a monthly allowance of food; other widows and girls stay in the rooms of the boyars' wives and daughters, and they receive their wearing apparel, and their food from the boyar's kitchen.

When these girls are grown up, the boyars marry them, and also the widows, to some one of their servants to whom they have taken a liking, but sometimes by force. The wedding takes place in the boyar's hall, according to the rank of the marrying parties; the food and festive dresses are furnished by the boyar. The girls are never married to any person outside the boyar's court, because both male and female servants are his perpetual serfs. In the boyar's house there

27

is an office for all domestic affairs, where an account is kept of income and expenses, and all the affairs of the servants and peasants are investigated and settled.

1671

STENKO RAZIN, THE GREAT COSSACK LEADER
by an Anonymous Authority

STENKA OR STENKO RAZIN was a famous cossack hero, a sort of Russian Robin Hood. From 1667 to 1671, he roused the underprivileged Russian peasants and his fellow cossacks of the Don to rise up against the government at Moscow and its policy of serfdom. Razin was not so much attacking the Tsar as he was the great landowners and officials whose cruel and rapacious behavior was inflicting hardship on the peasants. Protector of the weak and needy, Razin fought to "remove the constables from the towns and to go to Moscow against the landowners."

Betrayed by his own godfather, Razin was taken to Moscow, tortured and beheaded. Throughout this ordeal he behaved with magnificent courage, true to the hero-image that has made him famous throughout Russia in countless songs and folk tales.

The name *cossack* is said to be derived from the *Slavonian* word *Cossa* which signifies *spirit;* and it is thought, that that name was given to that people by reason of their agility or nimbleness.

The *Donsky-Cossacks* are those that have their habitation upon the famous River *Don* and belong to the Tsar or Emperor of *Moscovy* and *Russia,* to whom they yield a voluntary, rather than a compelled obedience. They are by the said Tsar endowed with many

Privileges, that if any slave run away from a *Russian* Nobleman or other Great Person, and come unto these *Cossacks*, the Proprietors lose their claim to them.

Of these *Donsky-Cossacks* was *Stenko Razin*, the person that four years since rose up in rebellion against the great Tsar *Alexis Michaelowitz*.

The beginning of his villainous attempt was his robbery upon the River *Volga*, An. 1667, where he took several great Boats laden with Commodities, belonging partly to Cloisters and Ecclesiasticks, partly to private Merchants. Thence he went to the Town *Jayck*, which he took by force, assisted by his *Cossacks*. Soon after he proceeded to the *Caspian Sea;* and from thence he returned to the *Volga*, where he did great mischief in giving interruption to Fishing, and in ruining many Houses. Thence he marched to the Town *Teock*, and further to the Frontiers of *Persia*, where he did great damage in giving interruption to Fishing, and in ruining many Houses.

To stop these cruel actions, the Waywode or Governor of *Astracan* sent some troops against him. Whereupon *Stenko* finding himself too weak, and apprehending a bad issue, asked pardon; to which, the said Governor returned this answer, that if he would desert from his violence and robbery, he doubted not that the Great Tsar would shew him mercy. He came with his companions to *Astracan,* almost sick and swelled, because having been a little before, upon a certain island in the *Caspian Sea,* beset by the Persians, they had been necessitated to drink salt-water. And he at length received pardon from the Tsar for his crimes and promised, that he and his Company would henceforth serve him with all faithfulness, nor exercise any robbery on the *Volga,* or the *Caspian Sea,* or elsewhere.

Stenko, being recovered, shewed his generosity to the Inhabitants of *Astracan.* For as he was walking through the Streets, he scattered among the people, store of Ducats and other Coyn he had robbed, and thereby was applauded by all; And then he, with his associates, went away to their own Countrey about the River *Don;* where he began to act afresh his villainy.

All sorts of imaginable mischievous devices were set on foot by *Stenko* to ruin the *Russian* Empire, and to seduce the common people.

Amongst other Artifices, he had prepared two ships, one of which was lined within round about with Red Velvet; and he gave out that in it was the Lord *Tsarawitz,* of glorious memory, *Alexis Alexewitz,* the Great Tsar's eldest Son; who yet in the year 1670 on the 17th of *January,* in the presence of his Father, in the Palace of *Mosco,* departed this life. *Stenko* boldly pretended that this Prince was yet alive and with him. And to colour this lye the better, he kept in the said ship a Youth of about 16 years of age, descended of one of the *Peregorsky Circassian* Princes, whom *Stenko* in his former depredations had taken prisoner. And he spread abroad, that the Lord *Tsarawitz* had made an escape from the violent hands of the Boyars and the great Lords, and taken his refuge to him; adding that he, *Stenko,* was come by order of the Great Tsar to put to death all the Boyars, Nobles, Senators, and other great ones, (that were near to his Majesty,) as Enemies and Traytors of their Countrey. By these base practises invented and pusht by *Stenko,* the ignorant people was inflamed to fight furiously, and those of them that were taken prisoners underwent death with a wonderful resolution, as being possessed with the perswasion of dying for a good cause.

By these arts *Stenko,* had so far advanced his design that the whole Tract of land about the *Volga* and farther up into the Countrey was engaged in this rebellion.

Hereupon the Great Tsar raised a great Army and sent it about the end of *September,* against the Enemy, of whom he met a party of Fifteen Thousand men, who though they fought resolutely and rallied three times, yet were at length beaten and put to flight, very many remaining dead upon the place and a great number being taken who were immediately executed. The place was terrible to behold, and had the resemblance of the Suburbs of Hell. Round about it were Gallows, each of which was loaded with Forty or Fifty Men. In another place lay many Beheaded and covered with Blood. Within the space of Three Months, there were by the Hands of Executioners put to death Eleven thousand Men, in a legal way, upon the hearing of Witnesses.

Stenko Razin, after that he had been routed, wandered up and down, until at length by the Captain *Cornelius Jacolowitz*, and those of the Donsky-Cossacks that had remained faithful to the Tsar, he was secured and brought to *Mosco*. This *Cornelius Jacolowitz* was god-father to *Stenko*, and always honored by him, as if he had been his Father, whence he never in the least imagined, that that person should contrive any mischief against him.

He was laid hold about *Tzanietza* and carried that long way of Two Hundred Miles to *Mosco*, entertained all along with the hopes that he should speak with the Great Tsar himself, and before him, by word of Mouth, plead his own Cause; he always imagining, that he had many things to say, very important to the Tsar to know.

Stenko coming within a mile of *Mosco*, the Waggon met him that had been made to bring him into the City according to his deserts. In the hind-part of it were erected the Gallows; himself was stripped of his Silken habit, which he had worn hitherto, and an old ragged Sute put upon him; and so was placed in the Waggon under the Gallows, with an Iron Chain about his Neck, fastened to the top of the same. Both his hands were locked fast to the Side-beams of the Gallows, and his Legs divaricated. His Brother *Frolko* was with an Iron Chain fastened to the Waggon, and went a foot on the side of it.

Thus entered *Stenko* with his Brother into the City of *Mosco*, Thousands of People, of great and mean condition, beholding them, and so fulfilling his Prophisie of the honor he should have in entering this Town. And though he comforted his Brother with this honor, yet himself standing in the Waggon looked on no body but held his Face continually downward.

They were both put to the torture. His Brother *Frolko* behaving himself most pitifully, *Stenko* went about to comfort him again, and said, that he must remember the good things he had enjoyed; that he had lived so long among his Friends with great credit and reputation, and had commanded thousands; and therefore he was now to bear this hard fortune with great patience.

Four days after that he was brought in, he was with his Brother carried to the place of Execution in the Cittadel. The Sentence of Death was read before him, wherein were expressed the Principal Villanies he had committed. He seemed not at all concerned, and spoke not a word but stooped. And when the Executioner was going to do his office, he crossed himeslf several times and thereupon he bowed his head thrice towards several places of the people assembled, saying *Prostie*, that is *Forgive me*. And presently he was laid down between two Beams, and his Right Arm cut off to his Elbow, and his Left Leg to the Knee. After this his Head was cut off with an Hatchet: all which was done with great speed in a very short time; *Stenko* gave not the least sigh, nor showed any sign of sense.

This was the end of *Stenko Razin*.

Arch-Abgel, Sept. 13/23, 1671, On Board of the Ship the Queen Esther.

1685

FROM ASTRAKHAN TO MOSCOW
by Father Avril, S.J.

DURING THE SEVENTEENTH CENTURY missionaries were needed for work in China in increasing numbers; but pirates, shipwreck and disease were killing most of the recruits that were being sent out by the sea route. Of six hundred who had been shipped out, not one hundred had arrived safely. Hearing that some travelers had managed to reach China by land through "Great Tartary," the Society of Jesus selected Father Avril to explore that route.

Embarking on the 13th of January, 1685, Father Avril arrived safely in Astrakhan but was forced to wait some months there before he was able to join a sleigh caravan that was bound for Moscow.

While waiting in Astrakhan for his caravan to assemble, Father Avril rode out to the mouth of the Volga River, "where the Muscovites have a great Fishery, which is one of the best Revenues which the Tsar has." This adventure is described in the first of the two following excerpts. Although methods of catching sturgeon have changed somewhat since 1685, the taste for the eggs of the sturgeon has remained unaltered. And today, as in Father Avril's time, caviar is one of Russia's most popular exports.

We had good sport in seeing the Fishermen catch Sturgeons, which is one of the greatest curiosities that ever I saw in my Life: and the manner of it is this.

The *Muscovites*, to make their best Advantage of the great plenty of Fish which the Caspian Sea distributes to all the Rivers that fall into it, have driven in long Poles of Timber, from one side to the other, in one of the channels of the *Volga*, which they thought most proper for their Fishery. However they do not shut up all the Passages so close, but that they leave one of each side for the Fish to swim up the River, and for the Vessels that return from *Persia*, and other places; a little above this first Barricade of Piles, they drive in others all a row, in the form of a Triangle, into which the Fish is easily carry'd by the violence of the Stream; tho when he is in, 'tis not only impossible for him to get out, but even to stir himself, as well by reason of the narrow compass of his Prison, as because of the huge bulk of his Body. In the mean time the Fishermen, who keep beating the Water to frighten the Fish into the Snare, visit their Entrenchments made on purpose twice a day, where they never miss of the Prey which they look for; which done, they thrust a great Hook through the Ears of the Fish, and having drawn him up just above Water, beat out his Brains with a great Club, to prevent his escape, or doing any other Mischief, should they preserve him alive in their Boats.

After this, they carry their Prize to the Banks of the Fishery, where they disembowel the Fish, and take out the Eggs, of which one single Sturgeon sometimes affords 'em so great a number, as weighs above two or three hundred Pound. This is that glutinous substance, so well known in Foreign Countries under the name of *Caviar*, which they prefer above all the rest. They salt it very carefully, and put it up with great care, to serve 'em in their Ragou's instead of Butter, which is forbidden 'em during Lent. As for the Body of the Fish, after they have cut it into Quarters, they squeeze out the Oyle, or else they pickle it up to be transported into all the Provinces of the Empire, or else into the Neighbouring Kingdoms, where they have an extraordinary vent for it.

But the pleasure that one took in this Fishing sport, was very much allay'd by the inconvenience of an Army of *Gnats* that swarm upon the *Volga*, a little before and after Sun set. Their Stings so terribly torment both Man and Beast, that I am easily induc'd to believe that of all the Plagues of *Egypt*, the Plague of the Flies was the most noisome and insupportable.

Therefore to secure themselves from this Vexation, Travellers wrap themselves over head and ears with a little Tent which they carry with 'em on purpose, so soon as they begin to feel 'em sting. But in regard we had made no provision against these formidable Enemies, we lay at their mercy all the while we staid in the *Volga:* so that when we came to Astrakan, we should have been taken for Lepers, or people that were troubl'd with a Dropsie, but that the Inhabitants were well acquainted wih the reason of the Wheals and Blisters that disfigur'd us.

The departure of the Caravan with which we had joyn'd our-selves, being fix'd upon the 10th of *December;* we set out all together in Sleds, which the Snow, already thick and Consolidated by the cold of the Weather, had render'd smooth and slippery; so that of all the Caravans that are made use of in *Europe,* there are none that I know of to be compar'd with this of Sleds, for swiftness and convenience.

This Machine, which is altogether in use over all the *Northern* parts; consists of two spars of Timber, which are as it were the Basis of it, and are very carefully plain'd under neath. These are joyn'd with several pieces of Wood laid athwart, and surrounded on ever side with the Bark of a Tree of sufficient Thickness, and just height to prevent the Snow from coming in. The bottom, which ought to be more solid, is plank'd very handsomely, and usually spread with a Mat, or a Bear's Skin, to keep out the wet; and within this Sled you may either sit or lye down, as you please your self. The *Muscovites* usually put their Beds in 'em, and lye in 'em almost all unready.

When you have made choice of your posture, you are presently cover'd with a large Carpet made on purpose, or with a furr'd Cover-let which you raise up, or else wrap your self over head and ears in, as you have a desire either to view the Country, or compose your self to Sleep. This sort of Cradle, which is about the bigness of a Man to lye conveniently along, is drawn by a Horse shod with Iron and Frost-nail'd, the Driver holding the Reins in his Hand, sitting at the Feet of the Person that rides in the Sled. Now, in regard this sort of

Machine glides without distinction over the Lakes, Marshes, and Rivers, that lie in the way; a Horse is so little tir'd with drawing, that after fifteen or twenty Leagues, that they usually travel every day, he shall be as fresh at his Journey's end, as when he comes out of the Stable in the Morning.

In such a Sled as this we travell'd to Moscow. The first three days we spent in passing through a Desert—above Forty Leagues in length; where we met with neither Tree, nor House, nor Cottage: so that we were forc'd to carry along with us our Wood, our Water, and our Forage, which was a little burdensome to our Horses. But this trouble was over, as soon as we had gain'd *Pinzer,* a little Village some few Leagues from this wild and uncultivated Plain.

The rest of our journey was pleasant and commodious enough; the Beauty of the Weather not a little contributing to render it delightful. For in regard the Winter days are exremely serene and clear in *Muscovy,* and for that the ways beside are as smooth as Looking-glass, all the Merchants make choice of this Season to drive their Trade, and by that means avoid the vast Expenses they would be otherwise forc'd to be at in transporting their Goods from place to place.

The Company that compos'd our Caravan, was in truth of very great advantage for the security of our Journey, because the Roads are very much infested with Robbers, that make no more of killing a Traveller, then of rifling him; but it was the Occasion that we made frequent stops by the way, where the Merchants have business to do; so that whereas it may be easily travell'd in twenty days, it took us up five whole weeks to pass between *Saratof* and *Moscow.*

We took care to get every night to some good Town, that we might not be put to lie in the open Air, which we never did in all that tedious Journey, but when we were engag'd in some of these dismal Forests which we could not cross in one day, and then we endur'd very little Hardship either. For in regard the Sled's which

36

are rang'd round about a great Fire that is presently kindl'd, are no less commodious, and as well clos'd up from the Air as most Houses you shall go into, you may sleep as warm and as quiet as in a Stove, nay more quietly then in a Country Stove, where Men and Beasts being higgledy, piggledy together, greatly hinder a man from taking his rest.

In this manner it was that we crost over vast Plains, of which I can say nothing more but that they were cover'd with Snow, and that of necessity they must be extremely fertile, considering the infinite number of Towns and Villages which I observ'd in these parts.

1701

TRAVELS INTO MUSCOVY
by Cornelis de Bruyn

CORNELIS DE BRUYN was a Dutch artist and a veteran traveler. One of his journeys lasted nineteen years; His trip to Russia was, as usual for him, a combination work-tourist affair. Sailing from The Hague on July 28th, 1701, he arrived at Archangel on September 3rd. A week later he set out with a friend on a visit to the Samoyeds, a primitive people who had settled around Archangel and in the cold, barren country to the east. "Nothing will be found here," says Mr. de Bruyn in his introduction to the book he published on his return to Holland, "but what I have seen with my own eyes, and have examined with the utmost Attention and Care." Using pen and sketching pencil with talent, as well as with the advertised "attention and care," he proves himself to be a perceptive and interesting guide to a little-known region and an even less-known people.

Upon the eleventh of this month I went up the river with my friend, to go to a country house he had, about 2 or 3 leagues from the city.

In our way, we landed at a wood, where we saw some *Samoëds*, which in the *Russian* tongue, signifies, *man-eaters*, or people that devour one another. They are almost all wild, and stretch along the sea coast quite to *Siberia*. Those, we now saw, were to the number of 7 or 8 men, and as many women, and were divided into five different tents; and had by them 6 or 7 dogs tied to as many stakes, who made a furious noise to us as we drew towards them. We found them, both men and women, employed in making of oars and bowls to throw water out of boats, as also little charms, and things of this kind, which they sell in the city and among the ships. They have leave to take what wood they want, for these uses, out of the forests. They are short of stature, and particularly the women, who have very small feet. They are of a sallow complexion, disagreeable to look at, having almost all of them long eyes, and bloated cheeks. They have their language peculiar to themselves, though they also understand the *Russian;* and are all clad alike in skins of the reindeer. They have an upper garment which hangs from the neck down to the knee, with the hair outermost and of different colours for the women, who by way of ornament, add slips of red and blue cloth. Their hair, which is very black, hangs about their ears like that of savages, and from time to time, they cut it by tufts at once. The women indeed do up a part of theirs, to which they hang small round pieces of copper, by a fillet of red cloth, to give them something of an air. They wear also a fur cap, white within, and black without. Some of them have their hair dishevelled like the men, and then it is difficult to distinguish them from the men, who very seldom have any beard, except a little upon the upper lip, which may, perhaps, proceed from their strange kind of diet. They wear also a kind of waistcoat and breeches of the same skin, with boots almost all white, in which women differ from the men in nothing but lifts or slips of black upon theirs. The thread they use is made of sinews of beasts, Instead of handkerchiefs or towels, they use very fine raspings or saw-dust of birch which they are never without, to wipe them when they sweat, or at meals, by way of a little cleanliness.

Their tents are made of the bark of trees, sewed together in long slips, which hang down to the ground, and keep out the weather. They are, however, open at the top, to let out the smoke, and therefore black there, though they are everywhere else yellow or reddish, being kept up by poles, whose tops appear above the rest of the tent. The way into these habitations is about 4 foot high, and covered with a great patch of the same bark, which they must lift up to go in and out, and the fire burns in the middle of them.

They feed upon the carcasses of oxen, sheep, horses and other carrion they find on the high-roads or that may be given them; or upon the guts and garbage of the same which they boil and eat without either bread or salt. While I was with them, I observed a great kettle upon the fire, full of these dainties, which none of them thought it worth while to skim, tho' the pot never wanted it more. The tent was also full of raw horse-flesh a horrid sight!

In one of the tents, I saw a child, about eight weeks old, lying in a cradle, or trough of yellow wood, not unlike the lid of a box. This cradle had a half hoop at the head, and was hung by two ropes upon a pole. It was covered over with grey cloth, tent fashion, but open at the top, and at the side, to take the child out and put it in. The child was wrapped up in cloths of the same colour, and bound about the breast with ropes or cords, as also about the middle and the feet; but its head was bare, as well as a part of the neck. As hideous as these people are in themselves, this child was agreeable enough, and even pretty white.

The tents are commonly full of skins of the rein-deer, which they use to sit upon. And this together with their manner of dressing their victuals, which for the most part is nothing but carrion, causes an intolerable stench. My friend, who sat by me, while I drew the child and the cradle, was so violently affected by it, that he bled at the nose, and was obliged to go out, tho' we had taken care to prepare ourselves with brandy and tobacco. Nor can it be at all surprising, for these people even in themselves smell very ill, which I attribute partly to their food and partly to their nastiness.

When they have a mind to marry, they look out for a woman they like, and bargain for her with her nearest relatives, just as we buy an horse or an ox. They give for a wife two or three or four reindeer, which are commonly reckoned at 15 or 20 Florins a-piece; a sum equivalent to which is sometimes paid, according as the agreement happens to be. Thus they take as many wives as they can maintain, tho' there are among them those who are contented with one. When a wife no longer pleases them, they have nothing to do but to send her back again to her relations that sold her, and they are obliged to take her again, the husband standing to the loss of the purchase he gave for her.

When their father dies or their mother, they keep their bones and never bury them; and I have been informed by eye-witnesses, that they even drown them when they are very far-advanced in years and of no farther use. In short, when a man is dead, they dress him just as when he was alive, put him into a pit, and cover him over with earth: and then, upon a tree, they hang up his bow, his quiver, his axe, his hatchet, his kettle, and whatever else was in use with him while he lived. In the same way they bury their women.

> After Archangel and his visit to the man-eaters, Mr. de Bruyn relaxed at "a party of pleasure" with well-to-do Russian friends who lived near Moscow. A convivial man, with a cultivated taste for food and an equally cultivated taste for the ladies, Mr. de Bruyn is always the artist, never so relaxed as to lose his eye for the significant detail and the pertinent fact.

Upon the whole there are but few curiosities in *Muscovy*. The great beauty of their country-houses, is in their fish-ponds, which are admirable. You have often two or three of them about a house, spacious and full of fish, which they are very fond of; and when any of their friends come to see them, the first thing they do, is to divert them with nets thrown into the water, and sometimes at a cast they shall catch as much fish as would fill 20 or 30 dishes and sometimes more.

I shall never forget a party of pleasure I had with some *Dutch* ladies, with whom I went to pay a visit to Mr. *Stresenof,* a rich man, who lived at the village of *Fackelorf,* 15 wersts [about 10 miles] from *Moscow,* where he received us very courteously. This gentleman had a handsome wife, a mighty good natured sort of woman, who did all she could to make us merry. The house was well built, full of fine apartments, and what is remarkable, it had a kitchen after the Dutch manner, a very neat one, where our ladies dressed some fish after our manner, though we had a good provision of cold meat, beside a score of dishes of fish in the *Russian* way with good sauces. After dinner they carried us into a room where hung several ropes by the beams. These were to swing in, the usual pastime of the country; and accordingly the Lady of the house took her turn at it, being swung by two waiting maids, who were pretty enough; while she was swinging she took a child in her lap and began to sing with her maids very agreeably, and in a most obliging manner; begging we would excuse her, assuring us she would have sent for music, had she had time enough. When we had thanked her for her favours, she carried us to the pond, and ordered them to get us some fish to carry fresh home with us. We took leave of our kind entertainers, and got into our coach extraordinarily well pleased with them.

Their manners are remarkable enough: when they pay a visit and go into a room, they do not say a word, but look about for the picture of some saint, wherewith their rooms are always hung; they make three low bows to it, and making several signs of the cross say *Gospodi Pomilus* "Lord have mercy on us;" or *Mier Esdom Zjeie-woesonon* "Peace be to this house, and to those that dwell therein;" again making signs of the Cross: then they salute the people of the

41

house, and speak to them. This is a custom they observe even when they go to see strangers, addressing themselves to the first picture they see, for fear they should not pay the first honours to God, as they ought.

When they entertain their friends, they sit down to table at ten in the morning, and part at one in the afternoon to go home to sleep, and this they do winter and summer.

1701

PETER THE GREAT MAKES SOME REFORMS
by Captain John Perry

WHEN PETER THE GREAT paid a visit to England in 1698 in order to make "his Observations on our Arts in building and equipping our Fleets," he engaged Captain John Perry to come to Russia and help him establish a fleet, as well as to assist the Russian engineers in making the rivers of the country navigable.

Captain Perry accepted the assignment, remaining in Russia for fourteen years. His main work was the building "of a Communication between the River Wolga and the Don." During this long stay in Russia, Captain Perry had plenty of time to observe the famous reforms inaugurated by Peter.

It had been the manner of the *Russes,* like the patriarchs of old, to wear long Beards hanging down upon their Bosoms, which they comb'd out with Pride, and kept smooth and fine, without one Hair to be diminished; they wore even the Upper Lip of that length, that if they drank at any time, their Beard dipp'd into the Cup, so that they were obliged to wipe it when they had done, altho' they wore the Hair of their Head cut short at the same time; it being the Custom only for the Popes or Priests, to wear the Hair of their Heads hanging down upon their Backs for Distinction sake. The *Tsar* therefore to reform this foolish Custom, and to make them look like other *Europeans,* ordered a Tax to be laid, on all Gentlemen, Merchants, and others of his Subjects (except the Priests and common Peasants, or Slaves) that they should each of them pay 100 Rubles per *Annum,* for the wearing of their Beards, and that even the common People should pay a Copeck at the Entrance of the Gates of any of the Towns or Cities of *Russia,* where a Person should be deputed at the Gate to receive it as often as they had Occasion to pass. This was looked upon to be little less than a Sin in the *Tsar,* a Breach of their Religion, and held to be a great Grievance for some Time, as more particularly by being brought in by the Strangers. But the Women liking their Husbands and Sweet-hearts the better, they are now for the most part pretty well reconciled to this Practice.

The *Tsar* came down to *Veronize,* where I was then on Service, and a great many of my Men that had worn their Beards all their lives, were now obliged to part with them, amongst which, one of the first that I met with just coming from the Hands of the Barber, was an old *Russ* Carpenter, who was a very good Workman with his Hatchet, and whom I had always had a Friendship for. I jested a little with him on this Occasion, telling him that he was become a young Man, and asked him what he had done with his Beard? Upon which he put his Hand in his Bosom and pull'd it out, and shew'd it to me; farther telling me, that when he came home, he would lay it up to have it put in his Coffin and buried along with him, that he might be able to give an Account of it to *St. Nicholas,* when he came to the other World; and that all his Brothers (meaning his Fellow-workmen who had been shaved that Day) had taken the same Care.

There was another thing also which the Women very well liked in these Regulations of the *Tsar*. It had been the Custom of *Russia*, in case of Marriages, that the Match used always to be made up between the Parents on each side, without any previous Meeting, Consent or Liking of one another, tho' they marry very young in that Countrey, sometimes when neither the Bride nor the Bridegroom are thirteen Years of Age, and therefore supposed not to be fit Judges for themselves. The Bridegroom on this Occasion was not to see or speak to the Bride but once before the Day that the Nuptials were to be performed; at which Meeting, the Friends on both sides were to come together at the Bride's Father's House, and then the Bride was to be brought out between her Maids into the Room where the Bridegroom was; and after a short Complement being made, she was to present the Bridegroom with a Dram of Brandy, or other Liquor, in Token of her Consent and Good liking for his Person. And afterwards all Care was to be taken that she was not to see the Bridegroom again until the Day of Marriage; and then she was to be carried with a Veil all over her Face, which was not to be uncover'd till she came into the Church. And thus this blind Bargain was made.

But the *Tsar* taking into his Consideration this unacceptable way of joining young People together without their own Approbation, which might in a very great measure be reckon'd to be the Occasion of that Discord and little Love which is shewn to one another afterwards, it being a thing common in *Russia* to beat their Wives in a most barbarous manner, very often so inhumanly that they die with the Blows; and yet they do not suffer for the Murther, being a thing interpreted by the Law to be done by way of Correction, and therefore not culpable. The Wives on the other hand being thus many times made desperate, murther their Husbands in Revenge for the ill Usage they receive; on which Occasion there is a Law made, that when they murther their Husbands, they are set alive in the Ground, standing upright, with the Earth fill'd about them, and only their Heads left just above the Earth, and a Watch set over them, that they shall not be relieved till they are starved to Death; which is a common Sight in that Countrey, and I have known them live sometimes seven or eight Days in this Posture. These sad Prospects made the *Tsar* in much Pity to his People, take away the occasion of these Cruelties as much as possible; and the forced Marriages being supposed to be one Cause thereof, made an Order that no young Couple should be marry'd together, without their own free Liking and Consent; and that all Persons should be admitted to visit and see each other at least six Weeks before they were married together. This new Order is so well approved of, and so very pleasing to the young People, that they begin to think much better of Foreigners, and to have a better liking of such other new Customs as the *Tsar* has introduced, than they ever did before, especially among the more knowing and better sort of People.

1710

THE TSAR PETER THE GREAT
by Charles Lord Witworth

WHEN M. DE MATUEOF, Peter the Great's minister in London, was arrested by two bailiffs for failing to pay his debts to some British tradesmen, the Tsar took the disgrace to his envoy as an insult to himself. He demanded immediate punishment of the offenders and threatened to avenge himself on any English merchants or subjects who happened to be in Russia at the time.

Queen Anne took it upon herself to answer her fellow ruler in a letter that is remarkable for its insight and tact: "There are insuperable difficulties with respect to the ancient and fundamental laws of the government of our people, which we fear do not permit so severe and rigorous a sentence to be given, as your Imperial Majesty at first seemed to expect in this case: And we persuade our Self that your Imperial Majesty, who are a Prince famous for clemency and exact justice, will not require us, *who are the guardian and protectress of the laws,* to inflict a punishment on our subjects, which the law does not empower us to do."

Together with the letter, Queen Anne dispatched Charles Witworth as Ambassador Extraordinary to deal personally with Peter. He managed to appease the Tsar and end the quarrel. Subsequently he continued in the Foreign Service and in 1721 was rewarded for his work by being created Baron Witworth of Galway in the kingdom of Ireland.

The present Tsar is in his thirty-eighth year, a handsome Prince, of a strong constitution, but of late much broke by irregular living, and other fatigues: He was very subject to convulsions, said to be the effects of poison from his sister Sophia in his youth, which made him shy of being seen, but of late they are much mended. He is extremely curious and diligent, and has further improved his Empire in ten years, than any other ever was, in ten times that space; and which is more surprising, without any education, without any foreign help, contrary to the intention of his people, clergy and chief ministers, but merely by the strength of his own genius, observation and example: He has gradually past through all the employments of the army, from a Drummer to Lieutenant General; of the fleet, from a common Seaman to Rear Admiral; and in his Ship-yards, from an ordinary Carpenter to Master-Builder: Farther particulars though agreeable, would be too long for this place; He is good-natured but very passionate, though by degrees he has learnt to constrain himself, except the heat of wine is added to his natural temper; he is certainly ambitious, though very modest in appearance; suspicious of other people; not over scrupulous in his engagements, or gratitude; violent in the first heat, irresolute on longer deliberation, not rapacious, but near in his temper and expence to extremity; he loves his soldiers, understands navigation, ship-building, fortification, and fire-working: He speaks High Dutch pretty readily, which is now growing to be the Court language. He is very particular in his way of living; when at Moscow he never lodges in the palace, but in a little wooden house built for him in the suburbs as Colonel of his guards: He has neither Court, equipage, or other distinction from a private officer except when he appears in public solemnities.

1762

THE JUNE REVOLUTION
by the Princess Daschkaw

PRINCESS EKATERINA ROMANOVNA DASCHKAW was born in St. Petersburg in 1744. She was related to the highest Russian aristocracy, and she tells in her memoirs that Empress Elizabeth "held me at the baptismal font." Her godfather was Grand Duke Peter, who became Tsar Peter III.

Brought up in the house of an uncle, the young princess spent a lonely childhood. Books were her great comfort, and she became something of a bluestocking. In the winter of 1759, when she was fifteen years old, she met the Grand Duke Peter and his wife, the Grand Duchess Catherine, at a supper in her uncle's house. The two brilliant young women took an immediate liking to each other. "At the time," says Princess Daschkaw, "I may venture to say there were not two women in the empire except the Grand Duchess and myself, who occupied themselves at all with serious reading; hence there was a point of mutual attraction; and as the graces of her manner were absolutely irresistible to all whom she chose to please, what must have been their effect on a young creature like myself."

In 1762 the Grand Duke Peter ascended the throne as Peter III.

He was a stupid, dissipated man, and it soon became apparent that his rule would be a disaster for Russia. A group of aristocratic conspirators, including Princess Daschkaw, plotted his overthrow. They staged a *coup d'état,* deposed Peter, and had Catherine declared Empress.

Partly because of her outstanding intellectual achievements and partly to reward her for her part in the "June Revolution," Catherine made Princess Daschkaw president of the Russian Academy, which she had been instrumental in founding.

It was in the afternoon of the 27th of June, that Gregory Orloff came to announce to me the arrest of Captain Passik. This latter had been with me the evening before, to warn me of the danger in which we were placed by the extreme impatience of the soldiers, especially the grenadiers, who spoke openly against Peter the Third, and loudly demanded to be led against the Holstein troops at Oranienbaum. In order to quiet the apprehensions of these two gentlemen, as well as to shew that I did not personally shrink from the danger before us, I desired them to repeat an assurance to their soldiers, as coming direct from me, that I had daily accounts from the empress, who was in perfect safety, and under no sort of restraint at Peterhoff, and that it was absolutely necessary that they should be tranquil and obedient to orders. Passik lost no time in conveying these injunctions to the soldiers, but in the confusion and tumult which prevailed, our secret came to the knowledge of the major of the Preobraginsky guards, who caused the immediate arrest of Passik, and thus by an apparently inauspicious, though in truth a most fortunate incident, hastened the discovery and happy catastrophe of our plot.

When Orloff came to my house with the news of this arrest, M. Panin was with me, who seemed to view this event in a far less serious light than I did. I, on the contrary, considered it the signal for taking some decided step. Orloff was desired to go immediately to the barracks of the regiment, and learn the particulars of Passik's confinement.

When Orloff was gone, I begged my uncle Panin to leave me, under pretense of wishing for some repose. But as soon as he had taken his departure, I covered myself up in a man's coat, and in this disguise set out on foot to the house of Rasloffleff.

I had not gone far on my way when I perceived a man on horseback in full gallop, riding as it were towards me. I know not why I came to imagine it one of the Orloffs, having never seen any of them but Gregory; but so strangely was I impressed with a persuasion of its being so, that I had courage enough to arrest the impetuosity of his course, calling out to him by that name. The horseman stopped short, and being told who it was that addressed him—"I was on my way to inform you, Princess," said he, "that Passik is under arrest as a prisoner of state. But why, madam, do you remain in the street? Suffer me to attend you home." "We are less observed where we are," said I, "than we should be at my house exposed to the curiosity of the servants. But, on the present occasion, a very few words will suffice. Go tell Rasloffleff, Lassounsky, Tchertkoff, and Bredichin, to repair without a moment's delay to their regiment, the Ismaeloffsky guards, and remain at their posts, in order to receive the empress at the suburbs of the city. Then, sir, do you, or one of your brothers, fly like lightning to Peterhoff, and from me entreat the empress to place herself instantly in a post carriage, which she will find in readyness, and drive to the quarters of the Ismaeloffsky guards, who are waiting to proclaim her sovereign, and to escort her into the capital."

Having dismissed Orloff, I returned home, but in such agitation of mind and spirits as left me little inclination to repose. I had ordered a suit of man's clothes to be in readyness for me this evening, but the tailor had not yet sent it. In order to repress the suspicions or curiosity of my servants, I went to bed, and in an hour afterwards I was alarmed by a violent knocking at the street door. Starting from my bed, and passing into the adjoining room, I desired that the person whoever it was might be admitted. A young stranger appeared

49

who announced himself to be the youngest Orloff. He came, he said, to ask if it was not too soon to send for the empress, who would be unnecessarily alarmed by a premature summons to Petersburg.

I could bear no more. "You have lost time already," said I, "which is most precious. And as to your fears of alarming the empress, rather let her be conveyed in a fainting fit to Petersburg, than expose her to the risk of spending her life in prison, or of sharing with us the scaffold. Tell, therefore, your brother to ride full speed to Peterhoff, and bring the empress into the city without a moment's delay; lest Peter the Third should have time to receive advice, and by arriving before her, should chance to frustrate a scheme which Heaven itself holds out to save our country as well as the empress."

After his departure, I became a prey to the most gloomy reflections. I longed to go forth and meet the empress; but the disappointment as to the suit of man's clothes was an evil spell which bound me to the solitude and inaction of my own chamber. This dreadful night, which appeared to me a whole life of suffering, at length passed away; but how shall I describe the transport with which I hailed that eventful morning when intelligence was brought to me that the empress had been ushered into the capital, and proclaimed head of the empire by the Ismaeloffsky guards, who were accompanying her to the church of Kazan followed by the rest of the military and the citizens, all eager to take the oath of allegiance.

It was now six o'clock. I ordered my maid to bring me a gala dress, and hastily, set out for the winter palace, where her majesty, I concluded, would take up her residence. It would be difficult to say how I contrived to reach it. The palace was so entirely encircled, and every approach to it so blocked up with soldiers who had flocked together from all parts of the city, and united themselves with the guard, that I was obliged to alight from my carriage, and endeavour to force my way through the crowd on foot. But no sooner was I recognised by some of the officers and soldiers, than I felt myself borne off the ground, and rapidly passed over the heads of all before me, who with one animated shout of approbation acknowledged me as their common friend, and welcomed me with a thousand blessings. At length safely set down in an antechamber, with my head giddy, a ruffle torn off, my robe tattered, and my whole dress in the utmost disorder, I hastened into her majesty's presence. We were soon in each other's arms. "Heaven be praised!" was all we could either of us for some moments utter.

Soon afterwards, when I observed that her majesty wore the ribbon of St. Catherine, and had not yet assumed that of St. Andrew, the highest order of the state—which no woman was entitled to receive, but of which as reigning sovereign she was grand mistress—I ran to M. Panin to borrow his blue ribbon, which I threw over her shoulder; and receiving the discarded insignia of St. Catherine, by her majesty's desire put them into my pocket.

After a slight repast, the empress proposed to move at the head of the troops to Peterhoff, and that I should accompany her on her expedition. For this purpose, choosing to equip herself in the uniform of the guards, she borrowed a suit from Captain Talitzen, and I, following her example, procured another from Lieutenant Pouschkin, two young officers about our respective sizes. These dresses, by the by, were the ancient national uniform of the Preobraginsky guards, and such as had been worn ever since the time of Peter the First, until superseded by the Prussian uniform introduced by Peter the Third. And it is a circumstance, worthy of notice, that the empress had on this morning scarcely entered the city, when the guards, as if by order, having thrown away their foreign costumes, appeared to a man in the ancient uniform of their country.

THE SLAVES OF RUSSIA
by William Richardson

WILLIAM RICHARDSON, the son of a minister, was born in a small town in Scotland. He received an excellent education, and at fourteen years of age entered the University of Glasgow. Here, after having won his M.A., he went on to study theology. In 1766, when Lord Cathcart was appointed Ambassador Extraordinary to the court of Catherine II, William Richardson was chosen to accompany the new envoy as both tutor to his young sons and secretary to Lord Cathcart. After four years in Russia, Richardson accompanied his oldest pupil home, and returned to the University of Glasgow. The following year, aided by Lord Cathcart's influence, he was appointed to the Chair of Humanity there, a post which he filled until he died at the age of seventy-two.

The peasants in Russia, that is to say, the greatest part of the subjects of this empire, are in a state of abject slavery; and are reckoned the property of the nobles to whom they belong, as much as their dogs and horses. Indeed, the wealth of a great man in Russia, is not computed by the extent of land he possesses, or by the quantity of grain he can bring to market, but by the number of his slaves. Those belonging to Prince Sherebatoff and constituting his fortune, are said to be no less in number than a hundred and twenty-seven thousand.

Every slave pays about a ruble (four shillings) yearly to his owner; and if he be in the way of making money, the tribute he makes is augmented. In general, every Russian nobleman allots to the peasants that belong to him, a certain portion of land to be cultivated by them, the produce of which, excepting what suffices for their own maintenance, is paid to the proprietor. Sometimes these slaves practice trades, or engage in traffic; and all such persons pay a much greater sum yearly to their owners, than is done by the labourer of the ground. In fact, a Russian peasant has no property; everything he possesses, even the miserable raiment that shelters him from the cold, may be seized by his master as his own. —A carpenter, being known to have made some money, was commanded by the rapacious steward of a rapacious Knaez [prince or duke], to give two hundred rubles to his owner. The man obeyed and brought the money in copper. "I must have it in silver," said the steward. The slave, denying that he had so much, was instantly scourged till he promised to fullfil the demand. He brought the silver, and the covetous superior retained both the silver and the copper. —You will easily conceive, that men in this situation, if they were ever able to improve their fortunes, will conceal their wealth and assume an external appearance of indigence and misery.

The owner has also the power of selling his slave, or of hiring his labour to other persons; and it happens sometimes that a Knaez, or Boyard [Boyar] shall give his slave to a neighbouring Boyard in exchange for a dog or a horse. The owner may also inflict on his slaves whatever punishment he pleases, and for any sort of offence. It is against the law, indeed, to put any of them to death; yet it happens, sometimes, that a poor slave dies of wounds he receives from a passionate and unrelenting superior. I have heard, that not long ago a lady at Moscow, the sister of Marischal S—, was convicted of having put to death upwards of seventy slaves, by scourging, and by inflicting on them other barbarous punishments. It was a matter of amusement with her to continue such modes of punishment as were whimsical and unusual. Such enormity, however, notwithstanding her rank, and the great power which the nobility have over their slaves, was not to pass with impunity. She was tried, was found guilty, and condemned to stand in the market-place with a label on her breast declaring the crime, and to be shut up in a dungeon. But she, who had felt no reluctance in making her fellow-creatures suffer the most inhuman torments, and had even amused herself with the variety of their sufferings, had such a sense of rank, and such lively feelings of her own disgrace, that pride, shame, and resentment deprived her of her reason. In truth, both the crime and the punishment seem to me strongly marked with the characters of barbarity.

As a Russian peasant has no property, can enjoy none of the fruits of his own labour more than is sufficient to preserve his existence, and can transmit nothing to his children but the inheritance of wretched bondage, he thinks of nothing beyond the present. You are not, of consequence, to expect among them much industry and exertion. Exposed to corporal punishment, and put on the footing of irrational animals, how can they possess the spirit and elevation of sentiment which distinguish the natives of a free state? Treated with so much inhumanity, how can they be humane? I am confident, that most of the defects which appear in their national character, are in consequence of the despotism of the Russian government.

1771

ADVENTURES OF A COSSACK SLAVE IN TARTARY
by Michaelow

WASSILIJ MICHAELOW was twenty-three years old when he enlisted in the cossack service. At that time, 1771, there was a great deal of unrest among the Kalmuck, Kirghiz and Kara-kalpak peoples, descendants of the Mongol invaders of the thirteenth century, who were now settled along the Volga.

In response to a report of a rebellion among the Kirghiz, seventeen cossacks, among them Wassilij Michaelow, were ordered to cross the Volga and investigate the rumor. They fell into a Kirghiz trap and some of the cossacks were taken prisoner, some were murdered, and others, including Michaelow, were sold into slavery.

In writing the story of his adventures Michaelow pictures himself as the hero of a fantastic series of adventures which ends happily with his return to Russia. The excerpt that follows gives a good picture of life as it was lived in a chaotic age in a region that is today the Kazakh Soviet Socialist Republic.

There being no market day at Kiwa, my master alighted at the house of an acquaintance, whom he had by chance met in the street. During summer and autumn the Kiwenses, like the Kalmucs and Kirghiz, live in temporary huts, which they usually erect near their cornfields and meadows: the other part of the year they live in houses of brick. The town itself is surrounded by walls of brick.

In the house at which we alighted, we were hospitably received and treated with Churek-cakes. For some time my master and his friend conversed in a low tone of voice. The two Karakalpaks soon after arose, and mounting their horses, left my master with our host, whose name was Ishnijas, and whose two brothers lived with him. As I was not wanted in the hut, I went out; took my saddle and placed it under a tree, and slept there till sun set. When I awoke, the wives and sisters of the household came to see me, pitied and endeavoured to comfort me, and gave me some Churek-cakes, which I ate with avidity.

My master passed the night in the house, and on the following day he said to me, "I shall exchange you in this house for another slave: you have no doubt seen in our way, not far hence, near the little river Atalik, a grove: I will there wait for you. Try to escape as soon as possible, and then we will return together, and at some future period I will take you to Oremburgh." I made no reply to this proposition but merely spit on the ground.

In Kiwa the Russian slaves are considered more valuable than the Persians. For this reason our landlord gave in exchange for me a young Persian named Safor and two Bucharian dresses. In order to terminate the exchange according to Kiwa custom, the most respectable people of the town were invited to a feast, which consisted of mutton and Plow (a well known Asiatic dish made of rice and butter, or grease. The Europeans call it Pilau.) "This Russian," said my new master, "I have received from Kinshal in exchange for Safor, and I have invited you, that you may all know it."

I had now the most humane master in the world: he conducted me about his house, and made me acquainted with every new object. The Kiwenses support themselves partly by manufactures and commerce, and partly by cultivating their fields, which furnish them with rice, millet, and wheat. My master and his family were employed in all these branches. A small piece of ground provided them abundantly with rice and corn. The women spun yarn, of which they made linen. Whatever they acquired by their industry was exchanged for cattle and different kinds of merchandise, and these again were bartered for other necessary articles. I had only some trifling domestic work to do, except that I occasionally assisted my master and his brothers in cultivating the land. In short I could not have desired to live more comfortably, but nevertheless I longed to go to Russia.

My master had two horses, some cows and sheep, which were sent to pasture in common with the cattle of the neighbours, and each of the owners alternately provided a person to guard them. I had lived three months with my new master, when the boy who used to guard our cattle fell sick, so that another was to be sent in his stead. "Wassilij," said my master, "our herdsman is ill: if he should not be better in eight or ten days, I will provide another herdsman: however, to-morrow you will drive our cattle to the pasture."

Having received from my hostess three Churek-cakes, I mounted one of the horses, and leading the other by the hand, drove the herd into the field. Not far from the town I unexpectedly met another herdsman whom I knew, and who was driving his sheep to the pasture: we agreed to guard our herds together, and as he was on foot, I gave up my other horse to him. About a verst and a half beyond us I perceived a lake, and, being very thirsty, I left the whole of the herd to the care of my companion, and rode to the lake: When I had reached it, I alighted, took some water in my hands and drank, and then wetted one of my Churek-cakes and ate it. The herdsman remaining much longer behind than I had expected, I was riding back to meet him, when I was met by two Tartars. I enquired if they had seen a boy upon a grey horse. The Tartars replied: "We have seen a boy not far off whose horse has run away." While the Tartars were speaking, the boy came running to me almost breathless, and related to me the accident. His horse, he said, had become shy, and, having neither saddle nor bridle, he was unable to manage it and had been thrown off. I left the boy to take care of the herd, and rode away in search of the horse. Supposing that it had run back to the stable, I galloped home, but the horse was not there. I then suspected it had returned to its former owner, a Karakalpak, of whom my master had lately purchased it, and as he did not live far from the town, I hastened there to make enquiries for it.

As the Karakalpaks lived towards the west, and I must take that direction if I returned to Russia, the thought suddenly occurred to me, that it was now possible to make my escape. Without much reflection, I hastened forwards, and rode about thirty versts without halting, till at length I reached the river *Atalik,* and the grove which had been pointed out to me by my late Kirghiz master. I rested there till towards evening and was preparing to continue my journey, when I saw before me three Karakalpaks, who were leading two horses. I overtook them and told them that I had been compelled to leave my master, because he was a miser, and would not allow his servants enough to eat.

57

The Karakalpaks listened to me without making any reply. At last one of them desired me to alight, and having himself mounted my horse, he rode towards a distant village and the other two made me follow on foot. We slept in the Steppe during the night, and on the following day about noon we arrived at the village where the other Karakalpak was waiting for us. The three Karakalpaks, who intended to rest for the day, said to each other, "If we take this slave farther with us, we may pay dearly for it: we had better deliver him up to the magistrate of the village, that he may be restored to his master."

I had scarcely heard these words when I devised a plan. I hastened to the magistrate of the place and told him that I was a Russian slave, and that my master lived at Kiwa, and was called Ishnijas: I added that I had the day before lost a grey horse, and that while I was searching for the horse, I overtook three Karakalpaks, and asked them if they had seen my horse? Who replied, "What do we care about your horse, come along with us; we will sell you to the Kirghiz." That they then dragged me from my horse and beat me most unmercifully and that I was now come before him to make my complaint.

The judge, well pleased with my behaviour, said he knew my master, and that he would send for him. He fulfilled his promise, and on the following day, towards evening, my master arrived with his second brother. When he saw me, he said, "Wassilij, how have you come hither?" I related to him my invented narrative. The good man sincerely pitied me, and said in a conciliatory manner, "You simpleton, why did you not return home? If the Usbecks, who you know live by plunder, had found you, they would certainly have carried you off." He then took from his wallet two cakes, which he gave me to eat while the supper was preparing.

It had already grown dark when we reached home. Our hostesses came to meet us on the road. They rejoiced at my return, and said in an endearing manner, "O you poor Wassilij; surely you must have suffered hunger with the Karakalpaks." The eldest then took me by the hand, and conducted me to the hut, where supper was now ready.

The sessions of the magistrate happening two days afterwards, the Karakalpaks related the occurrence to the magistrates, and swore by heaven and hell they had told the truth: but my deposition, being supported by my master, prevailed. The Karakalpaks were accordingly ordered to pay a fine of one sheep and four pieces of gold each worth about 2½ silver rubles.

1780s

ON RUSSIAN WOMEN
Anonymous

THE ANONYMOUS AUTHOR of the *Secret Memoirs of the Court of Petersburg,* from which the excerpt that follows was taken, lived in Russia for ten years during the latter part of Catherine II's reign (1762–1796). According to his publishers he lived in the capital, was well acquainted with court circles, and was "near the person of the empress." Since the book was translated from the French, he was in all probability a Frenchman. From his sophisticated comments on the manners of Petersburg society and the wit of his observations, it is clear that the anonymous writer was a man of the world, well equipped to compare the still-crude customs of the Russian city with the more-civilized European world that was his home.

I have already mentioned the revolting manner in which men are treated in Russia. A man's sensibility must be deadened, and his heart already hardened by spectacles of cruelty, for him to behold for a single moment, without indignation and horror, the punishments sometimes inflicted on slaves. But it must be confessed, it is still more revolting, to see women present, and even presiding at them, or sometimes inflicting the punishment themselves. I have been at tables, where, for some trifling fault, the master has coolly ordered a footman a hundred blows with a stick, as a mere matter of course; and he has been immediately conducted into the court, or into the anti-chamber only, in presence of the ladies, married and unmarried, who continued to eat and laugh while they heard the cries of the poor fellow being cudgelled.

I am not the first person by whom it has been observed, that in Russia the women are usually more spiteful, more cruel, and more barbarous than the men: and it is because they are still much more ignorant and more superstitious. They scarcely ever travel, are taught very little, and do nothing. Surrounded by slaves, to gratify or prevent their wishes, the Russian ladies spend their time lounging on a sofa or at a card-table. They are very seldom seen with a book in their hands, still seldomer with any kind of work, or attending to their domestic affairs. They, who have not been humanised by a foreign education, are still actual barbarians. Among them you may find such women as Juvenal describes, when he mentions one, who, speaking to a person that entreated her to spare a slave she was ordering to be punished, and conjured her to take pity on the man, answered: "Blockhead! is a slave a 'man?' " and another, that said to some friends who appeared frightened at some screams they heard while she was shewing them her jewels and trinkets, "It is nothing at all, it is only a man I have ordered to be flogged."

One who bears the title of princess, though she deserves not that of woman, by name K_____ky, exhibits a picture of crimes, rage, and turpitude, at which the reader would shudder. The outrages which she perpetrated on her slaves at Mosco, obliged the brother of this Tisiphone to send her to Petersburg, to save her from the vengeance of the people. He was at length compelled to forbid her to employ her own slaves as domestics, and she was fain to hire free persons, who never staid more than a day with her; and at length she was attended wholly by soldiers, who were sent to her house for the purpose.

I knew another lady of the court, who had in her bedchamber a sort of dark cage, in which she kept a slave, who dressed her hair. She took him out herself every day, as you would take a comb out of its case, in order to dress her head and immediately shut him up again, though seldom without his having had his ears boxed while she was at her toilette. The poor fellow had a bit of bread, a pitcher of water, a little stool, and a chamberpot in his box. He never saw day-light but while he was dressing the perriwig on the bald pate of his old keeper. This portable prison was kept close at her bed's head, and carried with her into the country. The slave spent three whole years in this *gehenna;* and when he made his reappearance he was frightful to look at, pale, bent, and withered like an old man. The chief motive of this strange barbarity was the wish of the old baggage to conceal from the world that she wore false hair: and for this she sequestered a man of eighteen from all human society, that he might renovate in secret her faded charms. The fasting and ill treatment which she made him endure besides, were to punish him for having attempted to escape, and because, in spite of all his art and care, she grew every day more old and ugly.

I do not mention these infamous acts, not more incredible than they are true, as general and characteristic of the Russian ladies: they are the crimes of individuals; but these crimes could not have been committed, except in Russia. In any other country, the relations, the friends, the acquaintances of the furies by whom they were perpetrated, would have looked upon them as singularities of their hunour; and the relations of the young man would have had a right to prefer a complaint against his mistress, and to demand justice.

What I have said of the Russian ladies among whom there are so many amiable and charming, I fear, will tend to excite too unfavorable an idea of them. Almost all of them are naturally witty, and by no means destitute of grace; their eyes, feet, and hands, are everything that could be wished; and there is an ease in their manners, a taste in their dress, and charm in their conversation, which are particularly agreeable.

These sprightly and amiable Russian ladies have taste for the arts. They laugh at the representation of a good comedy, readily perceive a satirical stroke, perfectly understand an equivoque, and applaud a brilliant line: but traits of sentiment appear lost on them, and I never saw one weep at a tragedy.

1786

A JOURNEY THROUGH THE CRIMEA
by Elizabeth, Lady Craven

ELIZABETH, LADY CRAVEN, was one of those intrepid Englishwomen whose adventures brighten the pages of travel history. In a series of letters to His Serene Highness, the Margrave of Brandenburg, Anspach and Bareith, whom she addresses as her "adopted brother," she reports on her journey through Russia and the Crimea to Constantinople. "Now I am on my way," she writes from Bologna, "I will see courts and people that few women have seen . . . few as the months are I can allow myself to run about in, I will enjoy them, I hope to my satisfaction and your amusement."

Enterprising, witty, observant and surely healthy, Lady Craven made light of her hardships. Although her spelling and punctuation frequently faltered, her spirit never did. It will not surprise anyone who reads her letters that Elizabeth, Lady Craven, eventually became Her Serene Highness the Margravine of Brandenburg, Anspach and Bareith.

Moscow, Feb. 29, 1786

I left my coach at Petersburgh, and hired for myself and my small suite, the carriages of the country, called Kibitkas; they are exactly like cradles, the head having windows to the front which let down; I can sit or lie down, and feel in one like a great child, very comfortably defended from the cold by pillows and blankets. These carriages are upon sledges, and where the road is good, this conveyance is comfortable and not fatiguing; but from the incredible quantities of sledges that go constantly upon the track of snow, it is worn in tracks like a road; and from the shaking and violent thumps the carriage receives, I am convinced the hardest head might be broken. I was overturned twice; the postillions I fancy are used to such accidents; for they get quietly off their horse, set the carriage up again, and never ask if the traveller is hurt. Their method of driving is singular: they sit behind three horses that are harnessed abreast—a shrill whistling noise, or a savage kind of shriek is the signal for the horses to set off, which they do full gallop; and when their pace slackens, the driver waves his right hand, shrieks or whistles, and the horses obey. I am told the whip is unmercifully used in the stables; I observed a postillion never strikes a horse in driving; which caused my astonishment at their being so tractable to the raising of a hand only. I would never advise a traveller to set out from Petersburgh as I have, just at the end of the carnaval; he might with some reason suppose it is a religious duty for the Russian peasant to be drunk; in most villages I saw a sledge loaded with young men and women in such a manner, that four horses would have been more proper to draw it than one, which wretched beast was obliged to fly with this noisy company up and down the village, which is generally composed of houses in straight rows on each side of the public road. The girls are dressed in their holiday-clothes, and some are beautiful, and do not look less so from various colored handkerchiefs tied over their forehead in a becoming and *pittoresque* manner. There is one particular piece of roguery practised after this diversion upon travellers, which ought to be put an end to: the horse employed on these festive occasions is generally upon the point of death; and the first post-horse that is wanted, that horse is harnessed to a kibitka in his place, because a traveller is obliged to pay the value of any horse that dies in his service. I had one that died thus, though I remonstrated upon his being put to the collar, seeing that he was dying, but unless I could have armed six servants with good cudgels, my arguments were as fruitless as those employed at the next post, to prove how unreasonable it was, that I should pay a great deal of money for a dead horse, that was dying when he was put to the carriage.

The Russian peasant is a fine, stout, straight, well-looking man; some of the women, as I said before, are uncommonly pretty; but the general whiteness of their teeth is something that cannot be conceived; it frequently happened that all the men of the village were in a circle around my carriage—and rows of the most beautiful oriental pearl cannot be more regular and white than their teeth. It is a matter of great astonishment to me how the infants outlive the treatment they receive, till they are able to crawl into the air; there is a kind of space or *entresol* over every stove, in which the husband, wife, and children lie the greatest part of the day, and where they sleep at night—the heat appeared to me so great that I have no conception how they bear it; but they were as much surprised at me for seeking a door or window in every house I was obliged to go into, as I could possibly be at their living in a manner without air. The children look all pale and sickly, till they are five or six years old. The houses and dresses of the peasants are by no means uncomfortable; the first is generally composed of wood, the latter of sheepskins; but trees laid horizontally one upon another makes a very strong wall, and the climate requires a warm skin for clothing. It might appear to English minds, that a people who are in a manner the property of their lord, suffer many of the afflictions that attend slavery; but the very circumstance of their persons being the property insures them the indulgence of their master for the preservation of their lives; and that master stands between them and the power of a despotic government or a brutal soldiery. Beside, my dear Sir, the invaluable advantage which these peasants have, as in paying annually a very small sum each, and cultivating as many acres of land as he thinks fit, his fortune depends entirely upon his own industry; each man only pays about the value of half a guinea a year. If his lord would raise this tax too high, or make their vassals suffer; misery and desertion would ruin his fortune, not theirs; it is true that a lord is obliged to give one man as a recruit yearly out of such a number; but it is one out of three or four hundred; so that notwithstanding this great empire is said not to be populated in proportion to the extent of it; when you reflect what a number of troops the Empress has, and these kept up by this method; the Russian people must be more numerous than strangers may imagine, in travelling through this country.

Yours affectionately,

E.C—

For centuries Russia had been engaged in sporadic border warfare with the Crimean Tartars, who were protected by the Ottoman Empire of which the Crimea had been a dependency since 1475. At last, in 1783, Potemkin decisively defeated the Tartar horsemen and the Crimea became a part of Catherine the Great's empire.

In 1786, at the time of Lady Craven's visit, the newly acquired country was still the "frontier," a colorful and exotic outpost with cossacks and Tartars taking the place of cowboys and Indians.

Karassbazer, April 4.

About six I passed the Tartar town af Karassbazar, lying to the left— and arrived at the general's house, a very good one, newly built for the reception of the Empress; the General Kokotchki, his brother the governor, and almost all the general officers were up and dressed upon the steps of the house. I found myself in my night-cap, a most tired and forlorn figure, in the midst of well-powdered men, and as many stars and ribbons around me as if I had been at a birthday at St. James's. I retired, but rose again at one, dressed and dined, and looked about me. This is a most rural and lovely spot, very well calculated to give the Empress a good opinion of her new kingdom, for so it may be called.

I had a Cossack chief presented to me, a soldier-like fine white-haired figure, he wore a riband and order the Empress had given set round with brilliants. In the evening, in an amazing large hall, several different bands of music played; and I heard the national songs of the Russian peasants, which are so singular that I cannot forbear endeavouring to give you some idea of them. One man stands in the midst of three or four, who make a circle round him; seven or eight more make a second round those; a third is composed of a greater number; the man in the middle of this group begins, and when he has sung one verse, the first circle accompany him, and then the second, till they become so animated, and the noise so great, that it was with difficulty the officers could stop them. What is very singular they sing in parts, and though the music is not much varied nor the tune fine, yet as some take thirds and fifths as their ear directs, in perfect harmony, it is by no means unpleasing. If you ask one of them why he does not sing the same note as the man before him, he does not know what you mean. The subject of these ballads are hunting, war, or counterfeiting the gradations between soberness into intoxication, and very diverting. As these singers were only young Russian peasants, they began with great timidity, but by little and little, ended in a kind of wild jollity, which made us all laugh very heartily.

In the evening I went with the governor and General to Karassbazar; and on the road saw a mock battle between the Cossacks. As I was not apprised beforehand, I confess the beginning of it astonished me very much. I saw the Cossack guard on each side of the carriage, spring from their stirrups, with their feet on the saddle and gallop away with a loud shriek. The General smiled at my astonished looks; and told me the Cossack Chief had ordered an entertainment for me, and desired me to get out and stand on the rising part of the down, facing that where a troop of Cossacks were posted, which I saw advancing with a slow pace; a detached Cossack of the adverse party approached the troop, and turning round sought his scattered companions who were in search like him of the little army; they approached, but not in a squadron, some on the left, some before, some behind the troop—a shriek—a pistol fired, were the signals of battle— the troop was obliged to divide in order to face an enemy that attacked it on all sides. The greatest scene of hurry and agility ensued; one had seized his enemy, pulled him off his horse, and was upon the point of stripping him, (A Cossack if he can avoid it, never kills his enemy before he has stripped him, because the spoils are his property, and he fears the blood should spoil the dress) when one of the prisoner's party came up, laid him to the ground, remounted his companion, and rode off with the horse of the first victor. Some flung themselves off their horses to tear their foe to the ground; alternately they pursued or were pursuing, their pikes, their pistols, their hangers all were made use of; and when the parties were completely engaged together; it was difficult to see all the adroit manoeuvers that passed.

Batcheserai, April 18.

On my way hither I dined at the Cossack Chief's post, and my entertainment was truly Cossack. A long table for thirty people; at one end a half-grown pig roasted whole; at the other a half-grown sheep, whole likewise; in the middle of the table an immense tureen of curdled milk; there were several side-dishes made for me and the

Russians, as well as the cook could imagine to our taste. The old warrior would fain have made me taste above thirty sorts of wine from his country, the borders of the Don; but I contented myself with three or four, and some were very good. After dinner from the windows, I saw a fine mock battle between the Cossacks; and I saw three Calmoucks, the ugliest, fiercest looking men imaginable, with their eyes set in their head, inclining down to their nose, and uncommonly square jaw-bones. These Calmoucks are so dexterous with bows and arrows that one killed a goose at a hundred paces, and the other broke an egg at fifty. The young Cossack officers tried their skill with them, but they were perfectly novices in comparison to them; they sung and danced, but their steps and their tones were equally insipid, void of grace and harmony.

When a Cossack is sick he drinks sour milk for a few days and that is the only remedy the Cossacks have for fevers.

Batchesserai is situated in so steep a valley, that some of the hanging pieces of rock seem ready to fall and crush the houses. There are five thousand Tartar inhabitants here; I do not believe there was a man left in his house, the streets being lined with Tartarian men on each side; their countenances were very singular, most of them kept their eyes on the ground as we passed; but some just looked up, and, as if they were afraid of seeing a woman's face uncovered, hastily cast their eyes downward again; some diverted at the novelty, looked and laughed very much. There is a great trade here of blades for swords, hangers, and knifes—I am assured many made here are not to be distinguished from those of Damascus.

The Khan's palace is an irregular building, the greatest part of it on one floor raised upon pillars of wood painted and gilt in a fanciful and lively manner, the arch, or last doorway, has fine proportions, a large inscription in gilt letters is the chief ornament. Court within court, and garden within garden, make a variety of apartments where the Khan walked from his own residence to the

Harem, which is spacious and higher than the other buildings. What I thought pretty enough was that several of the square places under his apartment were paved with marble, and have in the center fountains which play constantly. My room is a square of more than forty feet, having two rows of windows one above the other on three sides, and it was with difficulty I found a place to have my bed put up in.

I saw from the windows a kind of dome which raised my curiosity, and I am told that it is a monument built to the memory of a Christian wife, which the Khan loved so tenderly that he was inconsolable for her loss; and that he had placed it there, so that he might have the satisfaction of looking at the building which contained her remains. This Tartar Khan must have had a soul worthy of being loved by a Christian wife I think.

Adieu for the present, dear Sir,

E.C—

P.S. Wild asparagus grow in great plenty all over the peninsula, and a wild kind of horse-radish of an enormous size, and the strongest and best flavoured I ever tasted, the root is as long and as big as the stoutest leg you ever saw.

1788

THE RUSSIAN VILLAGE
by Chantreau

IN 1788, a Frenchman named Chantreau visited Russia from "commercial motives" and also to "see a new people" who were just in the process of welding themselves into a nation.

69

Chantreau entered Russia through Finland and went first to St. Petersburg and then to Moscow. He remained in Russia two years.

The villages to be met with every now and then upon the road [between St. Petersburg and Moscow], bear an uniform resemblance to one another. They have a single street formed by cottages of wood, hardly to be distinguished from houses of brick. These are good dwellings though constructed in the coarsest manner. They are built so as to resist the rigour of the climate. This is the principal aim of all who build. We noticed that the figure of them all was an oblong square, inclosing a court, having the look of a large barn, on the outside. In one of the corners of this inclosed space is the part of the house inhabited by the family, facing the street of the village, with an outside stair. This contains one, or at most two apartments. Beds are unknown in this country. In all the houses of the Russian peasants, there are never more than two for the heads of the family, in which they sleep with their clothes on, one at the head, another at the foot. The rest of the family lie on benches, on the ground, or more readily on the stove; a kind of brick-oven, which occupies almost a quarter of the room, and is flat on the top. Often the men, women, and children sleep promiscuously, without any regard to sex or condition. In some cottages we perceived a sort of frame, six or seven feet high, which they shift at pleasure from one end of the room to the other. In the center of this, there are several planks fixed horizontally above one another, upon which the members of the family sleep, often with their feet and head hanging; a posture very straining for strangers not accustomed to this kind of bed.

The great number of people, sometimes twenty, contained in this small space, added to the heat of the stove, renders the room, for the greater part of the time, inhabitable by none but the Russian peasants. It emits a suffocating smell, which custom alone makes supportable. This inconvenience is still greater in the houses, in which

70

there are no chimneys, and no outlet for the smoke. If during the night you wish to open the shutters for relief, and for restoring the air, a sharp frosty wind from without, soon forces you to prefer the heat and strong smell of the room, along with the smoke collected there. But, as we only went upon these ovens without continuing, and as we had to refresh outselves after the fatigues of the day, a profound sleep spared us all these disagreeable circumstances.

In the middle of each room was suspended to the ceiling, a vessel full of holy water and a lamp which is lighted only on grand occasions. It gives, or rather is intended to give light to a bog [a house saint], coarsely painted, and exactly like the village images that are to be found in Catholic countries. But, the honest Russians, when they rise and go to bed, do not for this omit to stand up before this bedaubed figure, for several minutes, performing numerous acts of worship, and the most devout, prostrating themselves on the ground. We noticed that the Bogs in almost all the villages, were a St. Nicholas, or a St. Alexander Newski.

The Russian peasants are very polite to one another. They lift their hats when they meet, bow frequently, and with much ceremony. In common conversation they speak with much action, never give over making gestures, and in particular express respect for their superiors in the most servile way.

The country people in Russia are well clothed, well lodged, and appear to have a plentiful and wholesome diet. Their rye bread at first offends the eye, but is a nourishing food, and when people are accustomed to it, there is nothing disagreeable in it. If they be hungry, they think it excellent, if they have travelled forty wersts, without getting anything, they think it delicious. The peasants season it, by a mixture of onions, oat-meal, carrots, green wheat and oil. Mushrooms are so common in this country, that they make a very considerable part of the diet of the inhabitants.

In Russia, fresh horses are only to be had at intervals of fifty wersts (upwards of thirty-six miles British). This is not too long a stage when the frost has made the roads smooth, and except in times of frost, there is no travelling in Russia. At least nobody will attempt it, if he be not compelled by imperious necessity. The peasants, who furnish post horses, are called *Jamshics*, and are obliged to find them to couriers and travellers at a very moderate rate. But as an indemnification, they are exempted from the capitation tax, and military service, and even enjoy certain privileges. But as they are so poorly paid for their horses, they give them only with reluctance. As soon as any person presents himself for a change of horses, they collect and dispute in a way that would amuse any one but a traveller bent on getting forward.

An hour is often not sufficient to settle the disputes of these peasants. The Post-master must often interfere, and compel them to cast lots. When a traveller is under the absolute necessity of making dispatch, besides his passport, he must be accompanied by a Russian soldier. Then the disputes among the Jamshics become less frequent, for it can be hardly imagined how much a soldier's cane shortens their controversies, how summarily it determines their debates, and how it brings out the horses the moment they are asked for. In these travels the passion of the Russians for singing may be noticed. The postillions sing the whole stage, the soldiers sing while on their march, and the peasants sing while engaged in their work; the taverns resound with spiritual songs, and at night a traveller arrives in the midst of songs, from all the neighbouring villages.

Once, while the Post-master was settling the disputes of the Jamshics, we amused ourselves with examining a plough and harrow at his door. We could not enough admire the workmanship. The plough was the simplest thing imaginable, and the harrow was nothing but a collection of trunks of young fir trees. If these instruments be attended with the least possible expense, it must be acknowledged at the same time, that they are weak and insufficient for tearing from the earth the fruits demanded of it; for they reach only to the surface, and in this climate the earth must be tormented, not caressed.

1789

THE BARSCHKIRES
by Chantreau

IBN-FOSLAN, writing at the beginning of the tenth century, describes the Bashkirs as "a war-like and idolatrous race." This is the first time they are mentioned in literature; but the description, "war-like," seems to have been accurate, for their Russian neighbors have not found them easy to live with. In 1556 the Bashkirs submitted for a time to Russian rule, but in 1676, 1707 and again from 1735 to 1741 they rose up in revolt. Finally, in 1786, they were freed from paying taxes, and this concession seems to have led to an improvement in their relations with Russia.

Bashkirs are described as having large heads, black hair, narrow eyes and flat foreheads. Strong and muscular, they are able to endure hard labor and to suffer privation. Their natural habitat is the slopes of the Ural Mountains and the neighboring plains. Today the Bashkirs have been incorporated into Soviet Russia as the Bashkir Autonomous Soviet Socialist Republic.

The *Barschkires,* more generally called *Barschkirians,* differ from wandering tribes in this; during winter they live in houses or huts, built in the Russian fashion. The principal part, which the family possesses, is furnished with large benches, which serve as beds. The chimney, of a conical form, and of the height of an ordinary man, is in the middle of this division, and so ill constructed, that they are very liable to smoke; consequently the *Barschkirians* are very subject to various complaints of the eyes.

The principal furniture of their hut is a bottle of an oblong shape, suspended near the chimney, and visited every hour of the day, because it contains their favorite drink, a mixture of sour milk and mead, which they call *Arjan*. So long as it lasts, they live merrily, and there is nothing they will not do to procure it. A stranger finds some difficulty in accustoming himself to this beverage. Yet we have seen Russian soldiers drink it as readily as *Barschkirians*.

In summer this people inhabit what the Russians call *Jurtes*. They are tents or cottages of felt, which, like the huts, have several divisions, and a chimney in the center. In the choice of a situation for a winter village, they pay more regard to shelter, and nearness of forage for their cattle, than to water, because they are accustomed to the use of snow water. A winter village contains from ten to fifty huts, but the summer encampment never exceeds twenty *Jurtes;* so that the large winter villages are divided into several summer camps.

Both sexes wear shirts of cloth made of nettles which have the same shape. They also wear, without any distinction, wide drawers, which descend to the ankle-bone, and a sort of slippers like people in the east. Both men and women wear a long gown. The men's gown is much larger, and generally of red cloth bordered with fur. They bind it round their middle with a girdle, or with the belt to which they fix their scymitar. The poor have a winter pelisse of sheepskin, and the rich wear a horseskin ordered in such a way, that the mane covers their backs and waves in the wind. The cap is of cloth, like the frustum of a cone, and ten inches high. By the rich it is usually ornamented with valuable furs. The gown of the wives is of fine cloth or silk. It is buttoned before, as far up as the neck, and fastened by a broad girdle, which the richer classes have made of steel. Their neck and throat are covered with a sort of shawl, on which are several rows of coins, or a string of shells. Their cap is a kind of monk's hood, which would disfigure them, if they were not gainers by hiding themselves. Their dress consists in concealment, for which we thought ourselves obliged to them. They all wear a bandeau on their forehead to distinguish them from girls and widows.

The *Barschkirians* are the most negligent and slovenly of the Tartars. In commerce they are the least intelligent; but, in return, they are the most hospitable, the most lively, and the most brave. They are also the merriest, especially if they have no uneasiness about providing for tomorrow, and few of them calculate beyond this term. Men and women are passionately fond of horses, the women especially. The most acceptable present that can be made them, is a fine horse-cloth. We have seen some of very valuable fur.

Their diversions at religious festivals, or at a marriage, consist in numerous libations of sour milk, singing, dancing, wrestling, and horse racing, in which they excel. In the songs they enumerate the achievements of their ancestors, or their own, and sometimes their amorous torments. These songs are always accompanied with gestures, which make them very theatrical. Among them, old age meets with the greatest respect. In their entertainment it occupies the place of honour, and the stranger to whom compliments are paid, is always set amongst the old men.

Although the *Barschkirians,* like most of the Tartars, are Mahometans; though they have their Mosques, their molahs, and their schools; they are not the less addicted to some superstitious practices, originating in paganism, or at least in the ignorance of the times when paganism prevailed. They have their sorcerers, whose knavery can be equalled only by the stupidity of those, who are the dupes. They challenge the devil, and pretend to fight desperately with him. If a credulous *Barschkirian* has by disease, or the severity of the season, lost one or two mares, he goes to consult the conjuror, who persuades him, that the devil has killed his mares, and that the next night he will go fight him, and drive him from his house. Next morning at break of day, the sorcerer appears with sweat on his brow, and all the external marks of a man who has been fighting. He assures him, for whom he has been fighting, that the enemy is conquered. The weak Tartar clasps him around the neck, thanks and entertains him, pays him, and returns to bed, calm and sure of having no more enemies. How many *Barschkirians* like him are to be found from pole to pole.

The *Barschkirians* have no Kan or King, since they became subject to the Russians. Their nobility also, which was numerous formerly, has been almost destroyed by intestine broils, and the wars they have had with Russia. At present, every tribe or *Woloste,* elects the chiefs within itself, two or more old men, whom they call *Starfschini* from *Starfschine,* which signifies department, or district. The nation of the *Barschkirians* is made up of thirty-six Wolostes, of which the total population is twenty-eight thousand families, or houses. Their language is a Tartar dialect, which is very different from that spoken at Kasan. The military service which they are bound to perform, and the only point in which the Russian yoke galls them, consists in furnishing in war times, three thousand cavalry, which form thirty troops of a hundred men each, usually armed with bow, arrows, a lance, a coat of mail, and a helmet. They are well mounted, are excellent horsemen, and still better archers. The greater part of them now have sabres, fusees, or pistols. A military corps belonging to this nation has a very singular appearance. Every horseman dresses himself as he pleases, and as he can. He has a led horse, which he spares for battle, and which carries his provisions, consisting of sour milk, and dried corn, which is ground into meal, with hand-mills, always following the army. With this meal they make a ball or bowl, which they swallow, and which serves them for bread. Every troop of a hundred horsemen has a standard of several colours, and these standards in the same regiment differ as much from one another, as the arms of the horsemen, who, on marches and battles, know neither ranks nor files, and yet fight not the worse for all this.

1799

A PARTY: SIBERIAN STYLE
by *Augustus von Kotzebue*

IN 1799, Augustus Friederich Ferdinand von Kotzebue, court dramatist to the Emperor of Germany and the prolific author of more than two hundred plays, set out for Russia with his Russian wife and three children on what was intended to be a happy vacation. At Polangen, a small town on the Russian border, Mr. von Kotzebue was arrested without being informed of the accusation against him, a not unusual event at the time. In spite of his protestations of innocence, he was torn from the arms of his weeping wife, placed in a carriage, and driven away under guard to Siberia. After a preliminary confinement at Tobolsk, he was taken to a small town called Kurgan. Here the celebrated playwright lived the life of the political refugee, joining good-naturedly with his fellow exiles in their pathetic efforts to amuse themselves and undoubtedly collecting plenty of dramatic material for future plays.

At four in the afternoon we came in sight of Kurgan. A single steeple raises its head above a group of mean-looking buildings. The town is situated on the elevated bank of the Tobol: it is surrounded with a naked and barren heath, which spreads itself on all sides, for several verstes, to the foot of some rising woodlands; it is intersected by a great number of lakes, choked up with reeds. The name of Kurgan, which signifies a *grave,* I had long considered as a bad omen.

After many turnings and windings, we came to a kind of flying-bridge, a mere raft, fastened at each end to the opposite shores of the Tobol, and exposed to all the violence of the waves. Every carriage that drove upon it caused it to sink considerably, and the greatest care was necessary to keep the emergent part in sight, without which the boatmen who stood on that part which was under water, would have no guide to direct them in crossing the ferry.

I have always thought, and I am convinced of the fact, that if a man be unfortunate, he will every where find friends: the arms, the hearts of men will open at his approach, in the most dreary wilderness, in the most remote corner of the universe! The good inhabitants of Kurgan are certainly of this description. I was invited to all their little feasts; every one would fain divide his pittance, and share his pleasures with me. On my arrival they did not know me as an author; but a paragraph which was inserted in the Moscow Gazette, relative to the brilliant successes of my pieces on the English stage, informed them of my literary existence, and served to increase that esteem which they had already evinced for me.

The following may serve as a sketch of the state of society of this place. The Assessor, Judas Nikitsch, celebrated the festival of his patron Saint, which it must be observed in Russia is a more important festival than a birthday. He came to me early in the morning, and invited me to his house, where, he said, I should meet all the principal people of the place. I went, and on my arrival was stunned by the noise of five men, whom they called *singers*. These men, turning their backs to the company, apply their right hands to their mouths to improve the sound of their voices, and make as loud a noise as possible in one corner of the room. This was the salutation given to every guest on entering the house. An immense table groaned under the weight of twenty dishes, but I could see neither plates nor chairs for the accommodation of the company. The whole had the appearance of a breakfast, which the Russians often give under the name of a *sacuschka*. The principal dishes were *pirogues,* not made of meat, as is usual, but of different kinds of fish. There were besides several dishes of soused fish, and pastry of many sorts. The master of the house carried a huge brandy bottle in his hand, eager to serve his guests, who frequently drank to his health, and, to my great surprise, without showing any signs of intoxication. There was no wine. Instead of wine our host presented us with mead; another rarity, and much esteemed here, as there are no bees in Siberia. Every guest, except myself, however, preferred brandy to this mead.

I expected every moment that another door would be thrown open, and that the company would sit down to table; but I expected in vain. The guests took their hats one after the other, and went away; and I felt it necessary to follow their example.

"Is the entertainment over?" said I to M. de Gravi, who stood near me.

"No," replied he; "the company are going home to take their naps, and at five o'clock they will be here again."

I returned at the appointed hour. The scene was then changed; the great table still occupied the centre of the room, but in the place of the pirogues, fish and brandy, it was covered with cakes, raisins, almonds, and a quantity of Chinese sweet-meats, several of which were of an exquisite flavour, and among which I remarked a dry conserve of apples cut into slices.

The mistress of the house, a young and charming woman, now made her appearance, and with her the ladies and daughters of the guests, in their old-fashioned dresses. Tea and French brandy were handed to the company, with punch, into which the *glukwa* berry was squeezed instead of lemons. Card tables were then set and the guests played at Boston as long as the brandy allowed them to distinguish the color of the cards. At supper-time every person retired as they had done at noon, and the entertainment closed.

1800

AN ENCOUNTER WITH SOME TARTARS
by Augustus von Kotzebue

AFTER HE HAD BEEN a year at Kurgan, Augustus von Kotzebue was
suddenly told that he had been pardoned. His release was as much
of a mystery to him as his arrest. Losing no time in making use of
his freedom, he hired a carriage and set out on the long drive to St.
Petersburg. The encounter with some Tartars which is described in
the excerpt that follows was only one of many little adventures that
enlivened the return journey.

Arrived in Petersburg, von Kotzebue was reunited with his
family, presented with an estate, and made director of the German
Theatre. It appeared that he had once written a comedy which fell
by good luck into the hands of the "mad tsar," Paul. This had
flattered Paul's vanity to such an extent that he had determined to
recall the dramatist. The original charges against von Kotzebue were
never definitely formulated but were thought to have arisen from a
vague fear that, as he was a writer and known to be something of a
liberal, he would be bound to disapprove of the autocracy under
which Russia suffered during the reign of the cruel and incalculable
Paul. When Paul was murdered in 1801, von Kotzebue and his
family returned to Weimar.

One evening, near sunset, the axle-tree of my carriage broke down,
when two or three Tartars immediately ran to my assistance. One of
them was a sort of carpenter. I stopped before his door, and learning
that the repairs would take up three hours, I desired my servant to
make some tea. The inside of the Tartar houses being very dirty, I
preferred passing the evening, which was exceedingly fine, before the
door; and having procured a table and a chair, I began to open my
travelling trunk to take out what was necessary to make my tea.
Curiosity had drawn all the inhabitants of the village about me, who
seemed to be totally ignorant of the use of utensils of luxury. An old
silk bed-gown, that my wife had often wished me to throw aside,

attracted their attention and admiration to such a degree, that every one of them was desirous to handle it.

But what delighted them to ecstasy was the looking-glass that lined the lid of my travelling box. They sat cowering in groups before it, laughed aloud at the sight of their own faces, and explained to one another, by droll gesticulations, their astonishment at seeing before them the country that lay behind them. I took the glass from the lid, and presented it to the carpenter's wife, who at first cast a look by stealth upon it, then grew more familiar with it, and at last admired herself with no small satisfaction, for she was very pretty. It appeared to me that the female Tartar peasants were not so scrupulous as the women of Cäsan in hiding their faces; at least all I saw here were without veils.

Tea being ready, I lighted my pipe, and sat myself down upon a pile of timber which stood opposite my carpenter's house. It was a picturesque nocturnal scene. A score of Tartars were seated about me, upon the rude steps formed by the beams of timber; at my feet a little fire was kindled, at which the carpenter was working; and across the way, close to the house, stood several women, girls, and children, who were too bashful to approach nearer.

By degrees a very singular conversation took place between me and the surrounding group. The moment they had discovered I was not a Russian, they took courage; I gained their confidence; they overwhelmed me with inquiries. They were ignorant of all Germany, except Prussia, and of that they had but very confused ideas. They had never heard of the name of France, of its revolution, nor its wars. Happy people!

A young woman whom the looking-glass had attracted so much, having in the mean while drawn nearer to us to profit by the conversation, I took an opportunity of asking her if polygamy was common among them; and it appeared that in all the village there were but two men who had more than one wife, and my carpenter was one of these. I was asked if I did not think it very agreeable to have several helpmates and several companions. Each by-stander strove to prove the advantages of polygamy. "When a man's wife grows old," said one of them, "she is associated with a younger woman." "When the old one is sad," added another, "the young one may smile and be merry."

"Very well," said I, "but does this arrangement please you females?" On saying this, I cast my eyes upon my pretty hostess. The by-standers explained what I said, as she scarcely understood a word of Russian, and when she had comprehended the question, she shook her head, as if she would say, "you are right to doubt it." After this she turned her eyes in a timid manner towards the door of her own house, where a woman of about forty, and of a crabbed look, probably her companion, was sitting. My eyes followed hers, and I was convinced that I had discovered a family secret.

I had evidently gained the good-will of this young woman, by the part I had taken in favour of her sex, for she soon after brought me a pot filled with eggs, which having placed upon the fire that was burning before me, she squatted down in such a manner that the flames reddened her countenance in a high degree: having boiled the eggs, she presented them to me upon a wooden dish.

As far as I have been able to observe the Tartar nation, I have found them frank, ambitious, quick in perception, of strong feelings and much addicted to revenge. The men are in general tall, stout, and hardy. With such faculties and dispositions, it is impossible that the conduct of the Russians towards them should produce any other effects than hatred. The Tartars are considered as the reprobate descendants of certain Finlandish colonies. They are used in the most cruel and ignominious manner. When any accident happens to a Russian on the road, he claims, as the bounden duty of a slave, the assistance of the first Tartar he meets, without condescending either to pay or thank him for his service. They even ridicule his prophet during the very time the man is at work for them, and while they themselves remain idle lookers-on. I have been present at a scene of this kind and I could observe the Tartar grow pale with anger, scarcely able to restrain his indignation.

As soon as the carriage was repaired, I prepared to depart. The carpenter received a trifle for his labour, but refused to take anything for his hospitality; and though this accident was far from being agreeable, as it impeded my journey, yet I cannot help congratulating myself on having employed the period of the delay in a very satisfactory manner.

1805

A LETTER FROM ELEANOR CAVANAGH
TO HER FATHER
by Eleanor Cavanagh

In the spring of 1803, Martha Wilmot, a young Irish gentlewoman of twenty-eight, set out for Russia to pay a visit to a friend. The friend was Princess Daschkaw, one of the most brilliant women in Russia, the friend of Voltaire, Diderot and Garrick and a former director of the Russian Academy in St. Petersburg.

In 1805, Martha Wilmot was joined by her sister Catherine, who was accompanied by her young Irish maid, Eleanor Cavanagh. In a letter to her father Eleanor describes with gusto, native wit and shrewd observation the fabulous life of the aristocracy as she experienced it at Troitskoe, Princess Daschkaw's estate eighty miles from Moscow.

October 4th, 1805

'Tis best my dear Father, to begin by mentioning that I am in Russia! Indeed where we are now (in a fine Country Place) is many a hundred mile from the first big Town we came to, that they call St Petersburg.

We were in a very pleasant Carriage the time of coming from Petersburg & travel'd in it for 8 days and 8 nights too. My Mistress bought me blankets & a Pillow (the same as her herself) and we had plenty of leather ones, so I'll engage I slept through the night fair enough & stretch'd at my full length because it was *quarely* made on purpose for travelling through the Night as well as the day. Well sure enough we *druve* right into Moscow, & 'Twas the handsomest Palace my hand ever seen, like half a round, & a big Temple at the top of stone steps! An Army, God knows, might live *unknownst* in the House! This was the Princess Daschkaw's.

From Moscow to the Country Palace where we are now and where we have been 3 weeks is more than 80 Mile. 'Twas like an Army when we left Moscow! Such loads of coaches, sarvants! I *druve* with the Princess's first maid Natasha. At night the Devil an Inn we came to, but a big Palace belonging to the Count! We sat very warm & pleasant, & then a sight of Maids belonging to the Palace came & kiss's us all round. I counted eleven of them, handsome looking girls enough, & mighty civil and nice. They made signs to us & we all follow'd them out of doors across a Garden to a *darling* place, & up we went up stairs till we got into a Play House. There was an auld Man with a Trumpet in his mouth & his two eyes looking at me. "Come up here" says Miss Anna Petrovna, the P^ss Niece (a fine young lady who lives with her always). "Come here" sais she. "I'm frightened Ma'am" sais I. Ogh then, such things as I seen nobody knows but my own self! I look'd thro' a little hole, & faith there I seen London & Petersburg & cart loads of grand Towns, but 'twas very *quair* Cork did not come any how! There were voices of live People talking out of little small Trumpets & singing, & doing every-thing like Christians. "Well to be sure," sais I, "Russia! & good luck to you, you are a comical place!" But this is not all, for when we went back to the Palace again there were 20 Musicians with Fiddles & Flutes & all sorts of Music playing *as fine as five pence!* "Carry me out" sais I. "What will come next?" As sure as I am a Gun I guess'd right enough, for the People came in & danc'd & sung all the time the Company was eating their Suppers, & they did not hinder us from standing at the Door to listen & look at all the fun. When supper was over I took notice that the Princess cross'd & bless'd herself & went away into another room & all the rest follow'd. So without more ado down all of us sat to the same Table & the men sarvants attended us, & I believe there were moe than 100 dishes. Fruit too of the finest sorts & kinds. We slept there & the next Morning we were up by six, & when the Ladies drank their Cups of Coffee I thought we were going off with ourselves, when my nose told my heart more dinner was coming; & sure enough tho' it was early there was smoking dishes of meat & fish & pies & fruit & wine just as if it was 4 o'clock & when the Quality had finish'd no blam'st to us all 18 Maid Sarvants if we did not wat out belly fulls! The laugh was not out of my mouth all the time, everything was so jolly & pleasant in itself.

That night we slept at an Inn belonging to the Princess herself, and the day after we came to where we are now, a grand elegant place! The name it goes by is Troitskoe; that is as much as to say *Trinity* in Russian, God save us! the first thing the Princess done was to go to the Chapel, a beautiful one she has of her own, & the priests gave her the Crucifix to kiss & sung psalms and burnt the blessed ashes, & then 2 Men at the Pillars of the Gate leading into the Lawn *stud* with a great loaf of black bread & a handful of salt on the top of it, & the Princess receiv'd it as an offering, & gave them her hand to kiss; & everyone was running to welcome her Home tho' she had been only away a couple of weeks. I was not here long when she sent me up a present of 3 yds of pink satin ribbon & 3 yds more of scarlet and yellow & a beautiful Silk Shawl border'd all round with white and blue. This was the day after a dance that her Maids gave and that she herself & all the Ladies came to look at. The Princess sent me over word that I must dance as well as the rest; & so my Mistress bid me, I was glad enough & I never *tuck* my feet from the ground till I danced down 5 of the Girls. No Men at all danced, only ourselves. That was not all, but in a little while afterwards she sent Maritshka & me a present of elegant Gowns, twill'd Calico; the whole piece was given between us, a pale green and blue stripe.

There is 16 villages all belonging to the Princess here, & them that lives in them comes to the number of 3,000 Men & Women, all her subjects and loving her as if she was their Mother. There is 200 servants lives in & out of the House. She one morning sent for me, and she was sitting in her own room about 7 o'clock in the Morn\ :sup:. "Ellen," sais she, "I believe you have none of the Money of my Country." "No Ma'am," sais I. "Well then," sais she (looking as good humor'd as anything) "you ought to know how to reckon, & so here are 20 roubles for you (each rouble is more than half a Crown), & they are in different kinds of Coin, you will learn to understand the value." Oh I forgot to tell you that she put the money into a blue Purse work'd with gold & tied with white ribbon & 5 gold Tassels. I never seen such a Purse, nor anything so handsome in my life! Another turn, Miss Anna Petrovna, the Princess's Niece, took me up to her own room! She does not know how to speak English, only "How do you do?" But she made signs to me, & I follow'd her & she went to her Desk and brought out a round ring with 3 rims of gold & put it on my finger, & then she laughed when I began to speak English to her, so I kissed her hand & made the best curtsey I could. And coming on she shew'd me a gown that one of her Maid Sarvants were embroidering in a frame; I never saw nicer work! & she has promised my Mistress that one of these days her Maid should teach me to work in the same way. Another of them is the elegantest mantua maker, and Miss Matty's too! They can sing & write & read & do many a thing very cleverly I'll engage.

We'll all be *laiving* this 13th of December for Moscow again where we are to stay three months in the same Palace of the Princess I talk'd to you about. And God knows I never see such a good Lady since ever I was born, nor so kind, nor so generous I've reason to say dear knows! Once every week there is a Play acted here in a nice little Play House belonging to the Princess. We are all given *laive* to go. 'Tis the Sarvants who act just for her amusement.

That's all, dear Father. I've put into the letter all I could think of.

& believe me your dutiful daughter
Eleanor Cavanagh

There's another thing to put in. One of the Maids made me a present of a Necklace, but my Mistress made me give it back again; for sais she (true enough) "what wou'd your Father say if you dizen'd yourself up with such nonsense!" So I gave it back again, & I never changes my own way of dressing at all. The weather is not a bit colder yet a while & the Stoves make the Halls & rooms much warmer than Fires. They are lit once a day. We breakfast early & then dine at the Princess's own Table as soon as the Ladies & Gentlemen go into the Drawingroom. 'Tis wonderful how early they dine, always between one & two o'clock, so that the Girls and myself sit down at four, but none of the Men Sarvants, & I'll engage we live like Queens! 'Tis the same at supper, for we have one like a hot Dinner at 10 o'clock afterwards.

THE BATTLE OF BORODINO
by Count Paul Grabbé

THE BATTLE OF BORODINO, although it ended in a Russian victory, was one of the bloodiest engagements in Russian history. Out of an army of a hundred and ten thousand men, Kutuzoff, the one-eyed Russian commander, lost forty-three thousand. It was this costly victory which led General Kutuzoff to adopt his famous delaying policy. Refusing to give battle, he retreated further and further into the interior of Russia, forcing the French army to overextend its lines so that it fell a prey to the Russian winter which in 1812 set in six weeks ahead of time. The French horse transport and supply system was disorganized by the cold. Constant Cossack harassment and peasant guerrillas did the rest, so that Napoleon and the remnants of his Grand Army were forced to retreat ignominiously.

Count Paul Grabbé was general aide-de-camp to the Emperor of Russia. During the war of 1812 he was attached to the staff of General Barclay de Tolly, and in this capacity he took part in the Battle of Borodino. The excerpt that follows is the account of the battle which he wrote into his memoirs. It is interesting that Tolstoy used Count Grabbé's memoirs as one of his chief sources in reconstructing the Battle of Borodino in his great novel, *War and Peace*.

At dawn of August 26, Prince Kutuzoff, surrounded by his suite, stood on a hill behind the right flank. All eyes were turned to the village of Borodino, which was about half a mile away from their position, separated from it by the river Kolotchea. It was occupied by the "Light Infantry" guard regiment. Barklay de Tolly considered it both dangerous and useless to try to hold this village and wanted to call back the light infantry without delay. The Duke of Wurtemburg disagreed with him. Kutuzoff listened to both of them in silence. Suddenly French rifle fire showered bullets on Borodino and the light infantry regiment, which, because of a dense fog, had not noticed the enemy's advance. Almost at once, the regiment was dislodged from its position with great losses; they rushed in disorder towards the bridge over the Kolotchea. The French followed them and did not give them time to destroy the bridge. At this moment I was sent to join the horse artillery with an order to occupy the hill that commanded the bridge and the area surrounding it. The order was carried out quickly, and soon the French, who were pursuing us, were showered with canister and grapeshot. Then the light infantry of Vuich repulsed and destroyed them. The bridge was also destroyed.

This prelude to the drama of Bordodino had not yet been completed, when the whole left flank was covered with a pall of smoke and thundered with gun fire. Soon the firing became one long, continuous roar. Yermolov and Count Kutaysov were eager to join Bagration, but for a long time Kutuzoff would not allow them to leave. However when one piece of bad news after the other began to arrive (the 2nd Army had suffered great losses fighting off violent enemy attacks; news of the death and wounding of many leaders, including Bagration himself), Prince Kutuzoff ordered Yermolov to the right flank to straighten matters out.

We had hardly come in line with the Rayevsky battery, when we saw gun carriages from this battery rushing towards us and our infantry retreating in disorder. Rayevsky's battery was in the hands of the French. Yermolov immediately turned his horse towards the battery, rallied the retreating mob and the Ufa regiment, and led them against the redoubt. The French were thrown back from the battery with bayonets. The interior of the redoubt was covered with their bodies.

To prevent us from taking advantage of our success, the enemy then bombarded us with their heavy artillery. This massive artillery bombardment showered us with canister and grapeshot, shells and grenades. As our positions formed a wedge, we were under heavy cross-fire. Disregarding their danger, our infantry stood in strict order on both sides of Rayevsky's battery. Yermolov sent me to tell the infantry that they could lie down in order to lessen the effects of the firing. But they remained standing and kept closing the gaps that were caused by casualties. There was neither bragging nor fear. They died silently. While I was giving Yermolov's order to one of the battalion commanders, he bent closer to me to hear me more easily. At that moment a shell smashed his head and I was spattered with his blood and brains.

Soon after I had returned to the battery, we saw Kutaysof's horse galloping across the field. Saddle and stirrups were covered with blood. Almost at the same moment, Prince Bagration, who was bleeding to death, and who had tried for some time to hide his fatal wound, was carried out. Orphaned without him, the 2nd Army which had lost nearly all its leaders through death or wounds, was held together solely by the desperate courage of the soldiers.

Having consolidated our position, Yermolov sent me to report the situation to Barklay de Tolly. I found him walking around under canister fire; he was eating something. He listened to me with a happy and smiling face, and asked me to congratulate Yermolov on his outstanding performance and to tell him that Dokhturov's corps was coming up to fortify the center.

The center and the left flank of our army were surrounded by an unbroken line of enemy guns. This was in preparation for the decisive attack. It was close to four o'clock, when massed infantry and cavalry moved towards our lines. Then an embittered and chaotic struggle began, in which infantry and artillery were intermingled. Each man fought as if victory depended on him alone. Our last cavalry reserves attacked and were mingled with the enemy cavalry. This was a decisive and grim moment in Russia's destiny. The scales of the battle seemed to be tipping in favour of the invaders. The central battery which had covered the field and filled the trenches with the bodies of the attacking French, were finally attacked from the rear and taken prisoner. Enemy cavalry raced madly over our fields crashing into the suites of the generals. Everything seemed open and in disorder. There were no reserves on hand, aside from a couple of regiments that were standing near the edge of the woods. Even though the enemy forces were in disarray, they had penetrated into our midst. Moreover, Napoleon still had strong reserves—his Imperial Guard—which we could see lined up in the distance, ready to descend on us, and crush any attack. Barklay de Tolly and Miloradovich were our guiding stars in these moments of chaotic battle; everybody was encouraged by them. Soon, the broken remnants of our regiments formed themselves into a new wall, prepared for a new battle. The momentary opportunity to achieve victory, was lost for the Emperor, who had dismounted and was watching the battle from a point directly in front of his guard regiments. Even to his experienced mind this battle was unusual for the intensity with which it was fought. He could not bring himself to commit his last reserves in order to widen the breach in the Russian lines. In my opinion this was the error which caused him to lose the victory that he had almost within his grasp.

Around five o'clock in the afternoon, the attacks ceased. Only some cannonading and an exchange of fire between the two lines kept on. It was clear that when the armies clashed, they had weakened each other to such an extent that nothing more of importance could be undertaken during the remainder of the day.

At last twilight came, soon followed by the long-awaited night. At last darkness covered the fields which were to be long remembered because of the holocaust that had taken place there.

THE BURNING OF MOSCOW
by General de Caulaincourt, Duke of Vicenza

ARMAND AUGUSTIN LOUIS, Marquis de Caulaincourt was born at Caulaincourt in Picardy on December 9th, 1773, and died in Paris on February 19th, 1827. The grandson and the son of generals, Armand entered the army at fourteen and became a career cavalry officer. At the age of twenty-nine, a veteran of fifteen years' service, he was named aide-de-camp to the first consul. When Napoleon became Emperor in 1804, Caulaincourt was appointed Master of Horse. One of his duties was to ride into battle with the Emperor, ready to give his horse to his chief should the need arise.

In 1807, Caulaincourt was sent to Russia as Ambassador Extraordinary. A man of the world, he hired the best chef in Russia, gave dinners for four hundred people, and made himself so agreeable that he became a very popular ambassador.

During Napoleon's disastrous Russian campaign, Caulaincourt was again at his chief's side, riding into battle with him, organizing his transport service, arranging for Napoleon's sudden appearances, and sharing his ignominious disappearance from the Russian scene.

The title of Duke of Vicenza was given Caulaincourt by Napoleon in 1808.

The Emperor retired early; everyone was fatigued and as anxious to rest as he was. At half past ten my valet, an energetic fellow who had been in my service during my embassy to Petersburg, woke me up with the news that for three quarters of an hour the city had been in flames. I had only to open my eyes to realize that this was so, for the fire was giving off so much light that it was bright enough to read in the middle of my room. I sprang from bed and sent my valet to wake the Grand Marshal, while I dressed. As the fire was spreading in the quarters farthest away from the Kremlin, we decided to send word to Mortier, to put the Guard under arms, and to let the Emperor sleep a little longer, as he had been extremely tired during the last few days.

I mounted my horse hurriedly to go and see what was happening. A stiff wind was blowing from the north, from the direction of the two points of conflagration that we could see, and was driving the flames towards the center, which made the blaze extraordinarily powerful. About half past twelve a third fire broke out a little to the west, and shortly afterwards a fourth, in another quarter—in each case in the direction of the wind, which had veered slightly towards the west. About four o'clock in the morning the conflagration was so widespread that we judged it necessary to wake the Emperor, who at once sent officers to find out how things really stood and discover whence these fires could be starting.

The troops were under arms; the few remaining inhabitants were fleeing their houses and gathering in the churches; there was nothing to be heard but lamentation. Search had been made for the fire-engines since the previous day, but some of them had been taken away and the rest put out of action. From different houses officers and soldiers brought *boutechnicks* and *moujiks,* who had been taken in the act of setting fire to inflammable material which had been laid in houses for the purpose of burning them down. The Poles reported that they had already caught some incendiaries and shot them; and they added, moreover, that from these men and from the inhabitants they had extracted the information that orders had been given by the Governor of the city and the police that the whole city should be burned during the night.

The Emperor was deeply concerned. Towards half-past nine he left the courtyard of the Kremlin on foot, just when two more incendiaries, caught in the act, were being brought in. They were in police uniform. When interrogated in the presence of the Emperor they repeated their declarations: their commanding officer had ordered them to burn everything. In the different quarters everything had been prepared for starting the fire—in accordance with orders from Governor Rostopchin, so they had been told. Many other depositions confirmed unmistakeably what they said. All the incendiaries were kept under observation; some were brought to judgment and eight or ten executed.

The conflagration continued to spread from the borders of the boroughs where it had started. The wind, which had veered slightly to the west, fanned the flames to a terrifying extent and carried enormous sparks to a distance, where they fell like a fiery deluge hundreds of yards away, setting fire to more houses and preventing the most intrepid from remaining in the neighbourhood with safety. The air was so hot, and the pine-wood sparks were so numerous, that the beams supporting the iron plates which formed the roof of the arsenal all caught fire. The roof of the Kremlin kitchen was only saved by men being placed with brooms and buckets to gather up the glowing fragments and moisten the beams. Only by superhuman efforts was the fire in the arsenal extinguished. The Emperor was there himself; his presence inspired the Guard to every exertion.

I hastened to the Court stables, where some of the Emperor's horses were stabled and the coronation coaches of the Tsar were kept. The utmost zeal, and I may add, the greatest courage on the part of the coachmen and grooms, were necessary to save the place; they clambered on to the roof and knocked off the cinders that fell there, whilst others worked two fire-engines which I had had put in order during the night. (They had been totally dismantled.) Everyone did his best to further the measures we took to check this devouring torrent of flame, but the air was charged with fire, we breathed nothing but smoke, and the stoutest lungs felt the strain after a time. The bridge to the south of the Kremlin was so heated by the fire and the sparks falling on it that it kept bursting into flames, although the Guards and the sappers in particular, made it a point of honour to preserve it. I stayed with some generals of the Guard and aides-de-camp of the Emperor, and we were forced to lend a hand and remain in the midst of this deluge of fire in order to spur on these half-roasted men. It was impossibe to stand more than a moment in one spot; the fur on the grenadiers' caps was singed.

The fire made such progress that the whole of the northern and the greater part of the western quarter was burned, together with the splendid playhouse and all the larger buildings. One drew breath in a sea of fire—and the westerly wind continued to blow. The flames spread continuously; it was impossible to predict where or when they would stop, as there was no means of staying them. The conflagration passed beyond the Kremlin; it seemed that the river would surely save all the district lying to the east.

About four o'clock in the afternoon, while the fire was still raging, the Emperor began to think that this great catastrophe might be connected with some movement of the enemy. The Emperor therefore gave the orders to leave the city, and forbade anything to be left within its walls.

1812

LETTER TO ALEXANDER I, TSAR OF RUSSIA
by Napoleon I, Emperor of France

OUTMANEUVERED by the Russian generals, who, refusing combat whenever possible, retreated further and further into their vast country, and faced with the imminent arrival of the Russian winter, Napoleon made a last desperate appeal to his "dear brother," the Tsar of Russia. Not so long before, after the battle of Tilsit, the two men had met and agreed to share the world between them. But Alexander, who had for years pursued a vacillating policy, stood firm in the crisis. He refused the peace Napoleon hinted at, and the Russian winter did the rest.

Shortly after dispatching his letter, the great Emperor Napoleon fled Russia, leaving his decimated army to straggle home in a disastrous retreat.

Moscow

September 20th, 1812

Monsieur mon Frère:

The beautiful and splendid city of Moscow no longer exists. Rostopchin has burnt it down. Four hundred incendiaries have been caught in the act; all declared they were starting fires by order of the Governor and of the Chief of Police: they were shot. The fire seems to have died out at last; three quarters of the houses have gone, a quarter remains. Such conduct is atrocious and aimless. Was the object to deprive us of a few resources? Well, those resources were in cellars that the fire did not reach. Even then the destruction of one of the most beautiful cities in the world, the work of centuries, for so slight an objective, is inconceivable. If I supposed that such things were being done under the orders of Your Majesty, I should not write this letter; but I hold it impossible that any one with the high principles of Your Majesty, such heart, such right feelings, could have authorized these excesses, unworthy as they are of a great sovereign and a great nation.

I have conducted the war against Your Majesty with no animosity. A line written to me before or after the last battle would have stopped my march, and I would gladly have foregone the advantage of entering Moscow. If anything of our old friendship remains, Your Majesty will take this letter in good part. In any case I shall deserve thanks for rendering this account of what is happening in Moscow.

1812–1813

RUSSIA AND THE WAR WITH NAPOLEON
by John Quincy Adams

JOHN QUINCY ADAMS, the son of the second President of the United States and himself its sixth President, served a long apprenticeship in the diplomatic service of his country before he achieved the highest office. As his father also spent many years abroad on diplomatic assignments, the young John Quincy attended schools in a variety of European countries.

When he was fourteen he was entrusted with his first mission, serving as private secretary to Francis Dana, the first American diplomat who was ever sent to St. Petersburg. By the time the younger Adams went to Russia again, this time as Minister in his own right, he had been given a variety of diplomatic assignments that took him to the Netherlands, Portugal and Berlin. In 1803 he had also served a term in the United States Senate.

A man of firm if austere character, a learned student of European affairs and a seasoned diplomat, John Quincy Adams brought great qualities to the fulfillment of his Russian mission.

15th [August]. They are organizing the new armament for the defence of the country, and the nobility of the governments of St. Petersburg and Moscow have given one man in ten of their peasants for the army. I saw many of them this morning, just in from the country, with one-horse wagons, and the families of the recruits taking leave of them. The number of volunteers is very great; and if they find it as easy to organize and discipline them as they find it to raise the men, there is little danger for the country to apprehend from the invasion under which it now suffers.

27th. Nothing is published respecting the late battles at or near Smolensk, of which there are now said to have been four. The letters from the officers assert the advantage to have been constantly on the Russian side, and wonder why the Commander-in-Chief, Barclay de Tolly, ordered the retreat. There is now an extraordinary clamor against the General. General Koutouzof, who was made a Prince after the Turkish peace, last week was appointed Commander-in-Chief of all the active armies, and left the city last Sunday night to go and take the command. The want of a single head of the Russian military force is a great misfortune to the country.

23d [September]. Rumours have been prevailing these three days that the French had been repulsed and the Emperor Napoleon mortally wounded. Mr. Harris paid us a visit in the evening, and told us that official accounts were now received that the Russian army had retired behind Moscow fifteen wersts, and that Moscow had been surrendered by a sort of capitulation to the French; that the King of Naples with eight thousand men took possession of the city on the fifteenth or sixteenth of this month, and that the Emperor Alexander was informed of it three days afterwards. The French Emperor with his great army had not entered Moscow, but was still in pursuit of the Russians. There has been no battle since that of the seventh, which Prince Koutouzof reported as a splendid victory, for which he was made a Field Marshal and received from the Emperor a present of a hundred thousand roubles. The result of this great Russian victory was to put the French in possession of Moscow.

30th. I had some further conversation with Mr. Laval. He says there are dreadful accounts of the burning of Moscow since the French entered it. There were two attempts made to burn the houses next to that in which *he* [Napoleon] had taken his quarters, and in consequence of which his troops set fire to the city in many places at once, and it is feared that the whole city may be destroyed. The Emperor Alexander, since the loss of Moscow, has said publicly at his own table, "Il n'y a qu'un coquin qui puisse prononcer actuellement le mot de paix." ["Only a knave could utter the word peace at this time."] His spirit stiffens with adversity. The situation of the French army in the midst of their triumphs is considered as absolutely desperate; it is supposed that Napoleon wishes to negotiate here. But the Emperor Alexander is not satisfied with the conduct of his generals. The defensive system is certainly painful and costly in its operation, and may perhaps not be calculated for a country situated like Russia. But it has not yet had its full trial. The time of real danger to the invader is now just commencing, and it is a species of warfare to which Napoleon is not accustomed, and for which he may not be prepared.

October 2nd. There is this day a publication here by authority, to assure the public that St. Petersburg is in no danger of being taken by the enemy, and explaining the motives for taking now the precaution of packing up and sending away the *necessary things* which they are doing in open day at the Hermitage and the public offices. There are also three encouraging bulletins of news from the army, and reports still more encouraging.

25th. I had visits from Mr. Montréal and from Mr. Laval, who has postponed his departure five days longer. He is not quite so sanguine as Löwenhielm that the French army will inevitably be destroyed, but he thinks the present prospects of the Russian cause superb. He still dreads the genius and resources of Napoleon more than they deserve. The accounts are so numerous and so uniform that his army is famishing, that he has proposed to Koutouzof an armistice, that his retreat through Smolensk is impossible, that they no longer are mere rumours.

27th. About noon this day the report of cannon from the fortress announced that important and pleasing intelligence from the armies had been received. The news was a great victory of Marshal Kou-touzof over the King of Naples, and the retaking of Moscow by General Wintzingerode's corps, though in achieving it Wintzingerode was himself taken prisoner.

28th. About noon I went to Kazan Church, and attended the Te Deum for Marshal Koutouzof's, or rather for General Benningsen's victory, and for the delivery of Moscow. The Duke of Serra Capriola and Baron Armfeldt were in the highest exultation of glory. Armfeldt had a letter from his son, who was with Benningsen at the battle, written the day after, in all the insolence of victory. Armfeldt went about reading it to anybody who would hear him. Without moving from where I stood, I heard him read it seven times.

4th. [November]. Went out to Ochta and dined at Mr. Krehmer's. There was much political conversation. The passions of almost all the politicians whom I now see are concentrated upon the head of one man. It seems almost universally to be considered that the destinies of mankind hang upon his life alone; and in proportion to the force of this sentiment is the ardour of his death. I know not how it has been with former conquerors during their lives, but I believe there never was a human being who united against himself such a mass of execration and abhorrence as this man has done. There is indeed, on the other hand, an admiration for him equally enthusiastic, as for every great conqueror there always must be; but I have never yet seen the person by whom he was regarded with affection.

25th. This morning. I received a notification from the Grand Master of the Ceremonies, Narishkin, that a Te Deum would be performed at the Cathedral Church at Kazan to return thanks for the defeat of the enemy's corps under the command of Marshals Davoust and Ney.

It is the greatest victory that the Russians have gained since the war commenced, and is perfectly decisive of the fate of the campaign and of the Emperor Napoleon's main army. It is now morally impossible that the remnant of them should escape. He is lost without resource. There have been rumours of internal commotions at Paris in circulation some time. The crisis is great and awful beyond all example. Almighty God, grant that it may turn to good! to peace! to the relief of mankind from the dreadful calamities of unbridled ambition!

8th. Mr. Montréal called upon me this morning. He told me there was a report circulating in the city that Bonaparte (he is now nothing more than plain Bonaparte) was killed. There is said to be a bulletin, on the other hand, from Admiral Tchitchagoff, admitting that Bonaparte, with seventy thousand men, had passed beyond him.

February 1st, 1813. At nine in the evening I went to Count Romanzoff's and had with him the conversation I had requested. I said I had heard that Count Lauriston was dead. There was such a report, he answered—that he had been found frozen to death in his carriage; and it was not improbable, as no mention of him was made among the Generals and Ministers who followed Napoleon upon his return to Paris. It is scarcely credible how complete the destruction of that immense army has been. The details surpassed everything that imagination could have anticipated. It was remarkable that at Dresden, the very spot which Napoleon had chosen for his point of departure, where in May last he had made such a pompous and ridiculous display of power, where he had assembled Emperors and Kings, and distributed their seats at the Elector's table, and published them in his gazettes, as if he had been there a monarch surrounded by his vassals—that exactly there, on his return, he entered the city in a single sledge, without servants, without guards. His very Mameluke had been frozen to death, and he was obliged to borrow four thousand louis of the Elector to continue his journey, and six shirts from his Minister. At Weimar he could not go any further in his sledge, which was broken, but borrowed the town carriage of Monsieur de Saint-Aignan, his Minister; and with this carriage and two soldiers lent him by the Elector of Saxony, he reached Paris.

1837–1838

AT THE COURT OF THE TSAR
by George Mifflin Dallas

GEORGE MIFFLIN DALLAS was United States Minister to Russia from 1837 to 1839. A friend describes him as being "at once stately and genial, robust and refined, and equipped not only with the learning which befits a scholar but also with all the accomplishments which add such charm to learning and to power." His diary shows him to be a shrewd observer as well as a man of considerable insight and common sense. The Tsar to whose court he was accredited was Nicholas I, who ruled from 1825–1855 and who was popularly known as "Ramrod Nick" because of his severity, his narrow conscience and his even narrower mind.

1837. November 1.—The commonest and most constantly recurring appearances are singular to our eye and taste. The streets afford at every step something for comment. Here, for instance comes a mere labourer. His covering is a sheepskin cloak, the wool inwards, lapping over in front, and kept together by a coarse and often colored girdle. It is dirty externally beyond conception, smeared black with grease and smells most offensively. He wears a hat of no shape, with the band drawn tight half-way in the crown. His feet are hid in a sort of matting, composed of strips about an inch wide and plaited in the form of a moccasin. His beard hangs a foot from his chin. His moustache is thick and conceals both lips, and his hair, coarse and matted, is cut close and round, just along the rim of his hat. His neck is entirely bare, and his skin is everywhere pallid, dark, and dusty. This is an exact delineation of the mass of the serfs or peasants whom you meet by thousands at work along the wharves, or on the public buildings, or at the highways. They are literally the "hewers of wood and drawers of water," and when in the former occupation have a huge, broad, short-handled hatchet stuck in their girdles; when in the latter, they move in pairs, carrying an enormous conical bucket, hanging from a bar of wood, which rests on a shoulder of each. The droschky driver covers his sheepskin with a blue woolen coat, has a black velvet collar and a scarlet belt. The domestic servants indulge in every variety of fanciful clothing. The shopkeeper is more staid in externals, but still prefers the girdled coat, and is inseparable from beard and moustache. The merchants, who are slowly rising in the social scale under the auspices of the existing autocrat, are assimilating to the merchants everywhere. Distinct from all these, distinct and domineering, are the military and nobles—the military, worthy of personal association only after their ranks have been winnowed; the nobles, spoiled by slavery, are fierce and despotic, but hospitable and patriotic.

1837. December 26.—I crossed and recrossed the Neva upon the ice to-day, and was amused by seeing the preparations made by a body of men for an extensive skating plain. Trees were planted in the ice on the line of demarcation; some benches were already stationed; the snow was shovelled and wheeled off, and through a hole cut water was procured and thrown in buckets over the appointed space, thus securing a clean and smooth surface.

On returning home, while walking along the English Quay, a single-horsed small sledge approached at a rapid pace, with apparently one of the numberless military officers in it, whom we see in all directions, enveloped in a light-blue cloak, and with cocked hat and feather, and speeding in the same unattended and simple manner. I did not notice, much less recognize, the person in the sledge until after he had made the usual gesture with his hand (putting it to the side of his hat by his forehead and there retaining it), and had nodded repeatedly at me, with smiles, as if endeavouring to make me know him. I had just time to whip off my hat and turn towards him most respectfully: it was the Emperor of all the Russias! He flew rapidly by, and I observed that all who were in his track seemed aware almost by instinct of his approach, and doffed their hats and caps instantly. The constitutional king, Louis Philippe, could not venture on this without the music of whistling bullets being awakened, and even a king or queen of England would run some risk of violence or rudeness. Yet such is the every-day practise of Nicholas the First. He is probably bold in the consciousness that he strives to do his duty, or the excessive degradation of his slaves prevents the least hazard of a generous aspiration and struggle for liberty.

1838. April 28.—The ice in the Neva gave way and started on its downward course at about ten o'clock to-day. At about five in the afternoon, the usual ceremony was performed by the Emperor drinking a tumbler of the water, filling the tumbler with pieces of gold for the benefit of the officer who handed it and ordering him to cross the river in his barge; the barge proceeds, cannon are fired when it is halfway, and again when over, and thenceforward the people are at liberty to use their wherries. The intercourse to-day between the city and the islands was suspended for eight hours; between six and seven

P.M. but few cakes of ice were perceptible. The bridge of boats was swung to one side at about noon, and will probably not be restored before to-morrow morning.

1838. April 29.—The weather was delightfully mild. The river, entirely free from ice, was again thronged with the fanciful summer boats.

1838. May 5.—The Emperor reviewed sixty thousand of his troops in the Champ-de-Mars at twelve o'clock to-day. We went there at about half past nine o'clock, and were early enough to witness the earliest preparations and every successive arrival of force. By half past eleven o'clock all the troops occupied their stations. The Emperor came on the ground accompanied by a numerous staff, a little after twelve o'clock, and cantered along the several fronts, saluted by a hurrah from every successive regiment, which he reciprocated by touching his hat. His progress awoke some fine music from the different bands. When he had finished, the Empress in an open landau with her three daughters, drawn by four bays with two postillions, reviewed the army in the same way. The two sovereigns then stationed themselves with their suite at the center of one side of the square and the troops marched by before them. His Majesty was so much gratified by the manner with which the soldiers performed their duty that he ordered two roubles to be paid each man. The precision and neatness of their movements well deserved the mark of approbation.

1840s

THE HUNT
by Leo N. Tolstoy

In *Childhood, Boyhood, Youth,* Leo Tolstoy (1828–1910), one of Russia's greatest novelists, writes of his own early life. The hunt which he describes in the pages that follow took place at Yasnaya Polyana, the Tolstoy estate in the Province of Tula. Tolstoy inherited Yasnaya Polyana on the death of his father, and it became his lifelong home. It was here that he wrote his great books, and it is interesting to note that, already in this early work, he dwells in loving detail on the familiar countryside and the "shining yellow" harvest fields that are so familiar to any reader of his novels. It is a measure of Tolstoy's genius that today, in Communist Russia, Yasnaya Polyana, the estate of the aristocrat author, is a national shrine.

The huntsman in chief, who was called Turka, rode in front on a dark gray Roman-nosed horse; he wore a shaggy cap, a huge horn over his shoulder, and a knife in his belt. From the man's fierce and gloomy exterior, one would sooner imagine that he was going to deadly conflict than on a hunting expedition. About the hind heels of his horse ran the hounds, clustered together in a many-hued, undulating pack. It was pitiful to contemplate the fate which befell any unfortunate dog who took it into his head to linger behind. His companion was forced to drag him along with great effort; and when he had succeeded in this, one of the huntsmen who rode in the rear never failed to give him a cut with his whip, saying, "To the pack with you!" When we emerged from the gates, papa ordered us and the huntsmen to ride along the road, but he himself turned into a field of rye.

The grain harvest was in full swing. The shining yellow field, extending farther than the eye could reach, was closed in on one side only by a lofty blue forest which seemed to me then a very distant and mysterious place, behind which the world came to an end, or some uninhabited region began. The whole field was covered with shocks of sheaves and with peoples. Here and there amid the tall rye, on some spot that had been reaped, the bended back of a reaper was visible, the swing of the ears as she laid them between her fingers, a woman in the shade, bending over a cradle, and scattered sheaves upon the stubble strewn with cornflowers. In another quarter, peasants in their shirt-sleeves, standing on carts, were loading the sheaves, and raising a dust in the dry, hot fields.

When we reached Kalinovoe (laburnum) woods, we found the carriage already there, and, beyond all our expectations, a one-horse cart, in the midst of which sat the butler. Under the hay we caught glimpses of a samovar, a cask with a form of ice-cream, and some other attractive parcels and baskets. It was impossible to make any mistake; there was to be tea, ice-cream, and fruit in the open air.

Turka came to this little meadow-encircled wood, halted, listened attentively to papa's minute directions (he never minded these directions, however, and did what seemed good to him) uncoupled the dogs, arranged the leashes in a leisurely manner, mounted his horse and disappeared behind the young birches. The first thing the hounds did on being released was to express their joy, by wagging their tails, shaking themselves, putting themselves in order; and then, after a little scamper, they smelled each other, wagged their tails again, and set off in various directions.

"Have you a handkerchief?" asked papa.

I pulled one from my pocket and showed it to him.

"Well, take that gray dog on your handkerchief. . . ."

"Zhiran?" I inquired with a knowing air.

"Yes, and run along the road. When you come to a little

meadow, stop and look about you; don't come back to me without a hare."

I wound my handkerchief about Zhiran's shaggy neck, and started at a headlong pace for the spot indicated to me.

Zhiran kept halting, pricking up his ears, and listening to the galloping of the huntsmen. I had not the strength to drag him from the spot, and I began to shout, "Catch him! Catch him!" Then Zhiran tore away with such force that I could hardly hold him, and I fell down more than once before I reached my post. Selecting a shady and level place at the root of a lofty oak, I lay down on the grass, placed Zhiran beside me, and waited. My imagination, as always happens in such cases, far outran reality. I fancied that I was already coursing my third hare, when the first hound gave tongue in the woods. Turka's voice rang loudly and with animation through the forest: the hound was whimpering, and its voice was more and more frequently audible. Another voice a bass joined in, then a third and a fourth. The voices ceased, and again they interrupted each other. The sounds grew gradually louder and more unbroken, and at length merged into one ringing, all-pervading roar. The meadow-encircled clump of trees was one mass of sound, and the hounds were burning with impatience.

When I heard that, I stiffened at my post. Fixing my eyes upon the edge of the woods, I smiled foolishly; the perspiration poured from me in streams, and although the drops tickled me as they ran down my chin, I did not wipe them off. It seemed to me that nothing could be more decisive than this moment. This attitude of expectancy was too unnatural to last long. The hounds poured into the edge of the woods, then they retreated from me; there was no hare. I began to look about. Zhiran was in the same state; at first he tugged and whimpered, then lay down beside me, put his nose upon my knees, and became quiet.

All at once Zhiran began to howl, and tugged with such force that I nearly fell over. I glanced about. Along the skirt of the woods skipped a hare, with one ear drooping, the other raised. The blood rushed to my head, and, forgetting everything for the moment, I shouted something in a wild voice, loosed my dog, and set out to run. But no sooner had I done this than my repentance began. The hare squatted, gave a leap, and I saw no more of him.

But what was my mortification, when, following the hounds, who came baying down the edge of the woods, Turka made his appearance from behind a bush! He perceived my mistake (which consisted in not *holding out*), and, casting a scornful glance upon me, he merely said, "Eh, bárin!" (Master). But you should have heard how he said it. It would have been pleasanter for me if he had hung me to his saddle like a hare.

For a long time I stood in deep despair, rooted to the spot. I did not call the dog, and only repeated as I beat my thighs, "Heavens, what have I done!"

I heard the hounds crossing in the distance; I heard them give tongue on the other side of the wood-island, and kill a hare, and Turka summoning the dogs with his long whip; but still I did not stir from the spot.

1844

THE SECRET POLICE
by Charles Frederick Henningsen

CHARLES HENNINGSEN was a long-time observer of the Russian scene. His book is based entirely on personal observation and upon the testimony of a variety of witnesses whose "on the spot" reports he was in a position to verify and guarantee.

At the time of Mr. Henningsen's residence in Russia, the Secret Police were extremely active; their agents were everywhere. From the time of the accession of Nicholas I in 1825, until 1843 when Mr. Henningsen wrote his book, he estimates that more than 250,000 people were sent into exile in Siberia and that of these three fifths had offended politically in some direct or indirect manner. No proof of guilt was required from the police, and with this policy of mass arrest many innocent men and women were involved; but, as the excerpt that follows shows, they were much too frightened of the authorities to demand redress.

In Russia, for several reigns past, there has existed a secret police. The Emperor Alexander, indeed, for one moment, suppressed it, but was speedily forced to re-establish it, by the dangers menacing his authority, and even his life.

Under the name of the Haute Police, Count Benkendorf, a Livonian nobleman, holds in his hands all the threads of his vast complicated machine. In him the Emperor Nicholas reposes unlimited confidence. The "high police," of which this man is grand master, is ostensibly established for the detection of all machinations against the state and the emperor—which, as in the idea of Louis the Fourteenth, are in Russia identified.

The very direction of this institution, as the Emperor Nicholas has organized it, unreservedly delegates to Count Benkendorf his absolute authority over all his subjects, amongst whom we must remember that even the imperial family is included. Every man in the empire is bound without question to obey the order of this vizier, as if it emanated from the imperial mouth—the mouth which makes laws as binding for sixty million subjects as if a nation had deliberately planned and pledged itself to obey them. If a sub-delegate of this grand master, distinguished by the livery of the secret police, present himself in the dead of night before a frontier palace, before the palace of an imperial prince, or the dwelling of the first magnate of the land, he must have instant admission to the governor, the

110

prince, or the noble—admission even to the bed of death and delirium, or into the nuptial chamber. He may drag any individual into a telega or kibitka, without asking any reason, without intimating why he is taken, whither he is going, or when he will return. Family, servants, and friends, must all keep a discreet silence on the event, and never even dare to ask, excepting after long groping their way through some influential channel, if ever, and when, he is to be restored to them.

When the individual so treated returns—if ever he returns—he has been "in the country," he has been "absent on business," frequently he is himself ignorant of the causes of his abduction; but he seldom confides what happened in the course of it, even to the ear of the most confidential intimacy.

There is a lady still living, who was stepping out of her carriage in her ball dress, when she was quietly handed into a sledge—her destination was Siberia. When the long journey was accomplished she was located—she knew not in what region or government—in a hut containing two rooms, each divided from the other, and leading into two separate yards, each a few paces square, and surrounded by a high wall. A sentinel was mounting guard outside the walls; her coarse food was brought in by a silent jailor, and here she remained for two years. At the expiration of this term, the door of the yard was one day opened, and a prisoner was thrust in to her, who turned out to be a Polish nobleman, who had been long confined in the adjoining cell, but was now removed to make room for another. In this room, or den, she lived with her unfortunate companion for twelve years more, ignorant alike of the spot of earth she was inhabiting and of the cause of her being banished thither. One morning, her door was thrown open, and a voice called for number so-and-so, by which, in the rare intervals of months and even years, they had been accustomed to address her. She stepped forward; the door was closed, and she was hurried into a sledge; she retraced the journey of many months, and one night found herself in the office of the grand master of police; a little cupboard was thrown open, and she was presented with the identical ball-dress which had been taken from her on the night of her exile. She was thenceforward at liberty.

This lady never knew the cause of her punishment or of its cessation. "And did you never make the inquiry?" "What, be so long in Siberia, and not yet have learned discretion!" "And what was said of your reappearance in society?" "Nothing; those who had known me formerly made no comment; to those who inquired, Who is Madame—? where is she from? it was simply answered, She has long been buried amidst her estates."

In the chief town of every government (the Russian empire being divided into governments, instead of departments or provinces,) there is a branch establishment of this institution, with a regular complement of avowed officers, besides a corps of mounted gendarmerie, although the whole force of the empire may naturally be called in, should they prove inefficient. Some thousands of officers, and agents, and brigades of this armed force, are thus exclusively devoted to this service, under the grand master's orders; but its secret agents, correspondents, and spies, direct and indirect, are supposed to outnumber many score of times those who wear its livery.

The passport-office is comprised in the institution of the high police; and through its intermedium every individual above the peasantry is registered. Annexed to the duplicate of his registry, is a compilation of all the reports, collected by all the spies who have come across him during his life, with their original observations, notes, and denunciations, all arranged with such admirable order and regularity, that in St. Petersburg and Moscow, within a few hours, the superintendent of police can become acquainted with the most secret actions of his life, together with the opinions he is supposed to entertain, or, at least, the sentiments he has avowed. There is thus many an individual who imagines himself utterly beneath the notice of the government, to whose name, in its black registry, are appended whole manuscript volumes upon volumes of secret information. Cordial acquaintances, dear friends, servants, and slaves, and too often relatives, have consciously or unconsciously contributed to swell the mass.

"Man forgets and God forgives," whispered a Russian, "but the secret police neither forgets nor forgives."

1852

A LETTER TO MADAME VIARDOT
by Ivan Turgenev

IVAN SERGEEVICH TURGENEV (1818–1883) was one of Russia's greatest novelists and the first one to be read widely abroad. Turgenev lived in France for many years, and during a stay there he met a famous singer, Pauline Garcia (Madame Viardot), with whom he fell madly in love. His mother disapproved of the affair and disinherited him. Nothing daunted, Turgenev adjusted his way of life to a Bohemian style and remained in love with Madame Viardot until he died. Unfortunately the famous singer did not return his affection but merely tolerated her admirer.

In 1952, while Turgenev was in Russia on one of his periodic visits, Gogol died. Turgenev wrote an article for the *Moscow Gazette* in commemoration of his fellow writer. This, although it had been given the sanction of the censor, was used as a pretext to discipline Turgenev for an earlier work, *A Sportsman's Sketches*. In this book, sometimes called the *Uncle Tom's Cabin* of Russia, Turgenev had drawn a picture of the hardships suffered by the Russian peasant, and it had aroused public opinion which did much to hasten the freeing of the serfs.

113

Turgenev was sentenced to a month's imprisonment, and although his stay in jail was made tolerable by the two daughters of the superintendent, who managed to get special treatment for the writer whose work they admired, Turgenev hurried off to France as soon as he had regained his freedom.

St. Petersburg

May 1/13, 1852

My dear friends,—This letter will be brought to you by someone who leaves here in a few days' time, or rather he will send it to Paris, after having crossed the frontier, in order that I may speak to you with a certain amount of frankness and without fear of police curiosity.

I will begin by telling you that if I didn't leave St. Petersburg a month ago, it was quite against my will. I am under arrest, by the Emperor's order, in a house belonging to an officer of police, for having printed an article of a few lines on Gogol. This was only a pretext, the article being in itself unimportant. I have been looked askance upon for some time, and they have seized on the first opportunity which turned up. I do not complain of the Emperor; the matter has been so wilfully misrepresented to him that he couldn't well have done otherwise. The fact is the authorities wish to put an end to all that was being said about Gogol's death, and they were not sorry at the same time to put a stopper on my literary activity.

In a fortnight's time I shall be sent to the country, where I am to remain until further orders. All this is not cheerful, as you may see. Nevertheless I am bound to say that I am very kindly treated. I have a good room, books, and I am allowed to write. I was allowed to see people during the first few days; now it is forbidden because too many came. Misfortune does not put *friends* to flight even in Russia. The actual misfortune, to tell the truth, is not very great; the year 1852 will have no spring for me, that's all. Just now I have only one wish, and that is that they will let me come and go freely in the interior of Russia. I hope they will not refuse me that. The Heir-apparent is very kindly disposed. I have written him a letter from which I expect some good to result; the Emperor, you know, has gone away.

They sealed all my papers, or rather they put seals on the doors of my rooms—which they removed ten days later without having examined anything. Probably they knew that they would find nothing of a forbidden nature. I must confess I am a good deal bored in my hole. I am taking advantage of this enforced leisure to work at Polish, which I began to learn six weeks ago. I have fourteen days of confinement left me. You may imagine how I count them!

My health is good, but I am ridiculously aged. I could send you a lock of white hair, without exaggeration, yet I don't lose heart. There is sport waiting for me in the country! Then I'm going to put my affairs in order. I shall go on with my studies of the Russian people, the strangest, the most astonishing people on the face of the earth. I shall work at my novel with all the more freedom of mind because it is not destined to pass through the Censor's clutches. My arrest will probably make the publication of my work in Moscow impossible. I am sorry for it, but what can one do?

Goodbye, dear friend. Be happy and your happiness will make me as content as it is possible for me to be. Goodbye.

Iv. Turgenev

1854

THE CHARGE OF THE LIGHT BRIGADE
by General Sir Evelyn Wood, V.C.

TENNYSON'S POEM, "The Charge of the Light Brigade," has long
been a favorite with patriotic Englishmen and their American cous-
ins. It celebrates the desperate charge of an English brigade of light
cavalry against the Russians at the Battle of Balaklava in the Crimean War, fought on October 25th, 1854.

General Sir Evelyn Wood, who gives the account of the battle
that follows, was not an actual eyewitness of the engagement; but he
joined the 13th Light Dragoons, the "Light Brigade," before the end
of the war. Talking to many of the survivors of that disastrous
charge, he was able to piece together the story of tragic error and unworthy rivalries that resulted in the death or wounding of more
than two-thirds of the original company of 673.

Although I did not see the Light brigade charge, of which no Briton
can think without a quickened feeling in his heart, yet having enjoyed exceptional opportunities of associating with some of the most
prominent actors in that dramatic scene, I venture to suggest that the
chivalrous errors, which, if they did not induce the charge, yet contributed to the heavy loss, cannot justly be attributed to only one or
two men.

The two leading regiments in the charge were the 13th Light
Dragoons and the 17th Lancers. I joined the former before the end
of the war, and the latter in the time of the Sepoy Mutiny, and thus
had many opportunities of hearing at first hand not only of the inci-
dence of that glorious half-hour, but also of the events of the previous
six months.

When the Army went to the East, our cavalry officers held a very
high opinion of the possibilities of their Arm, combined with but

little knowledge and a lesser opinion of the value of the other branches of the Service. When therefore, 1100 Sabres looked on while the Infantry stormed the heights overlooking Bourliouk on the Alma, the irritation amongst the ardent horsemen was intense, and this was not soothed until they showed that no task was too great for their burning courage. The General who was supposed to have Lord Raglan's ear at this time, wrote on the 26th of October, "There has been much dissatisfaction expressed (whether right or wrong) at the way in which our cavalry has been managed, even the cavalry officers themselves considering it has not been forward enough."

The Light brigade had an hour or two previously been looking on while their comrades in the Heavy brigade achieved one of the most brilliant cavalry victories ever recorded, and officers were naturally eager to emulate such a deed. This state of feeling explains, to a certain extent, how two proud, brave leaders, with no knowledge of war, were easily led into attempting to execute an order of which they both disapproved.

Lord Lucan, the Divisional cavalry leader on receipt of an order brought by Captain Nolan freely criticized Lord Raglan's instructions. The order reiterated a somewhat similar command sent down previously: "Lord Raglan wishes the cavalry to advance rapidly to the front, and try to prevent the enemy carrying away the guns."

From the spot where Lord Lucan received this order, no Russians were visible, and he asked sharply, "Attack, sir! Attack what guns?" The General considered that Captain Nolan replied in an insulting tone as he said, pointing in an Easterly direction, "There, my Lord, is your enemy, and there are your guns."

The brigade moved forward at the trot. Shortly after it advanced, Captain Nolan was seen galloping across the front, shouting, and pointing with his sword. Lord Cardigan, not realizing what Nolan was endeavouring to convey, regarded this as an unwarrantable interference with the direction of the brigade; and Nolan was unable to give any further information for the first shell, bursting just in front of his horse, tore away part of the brave Hussar's chest.

After the brigade had been a few moment's in motion, it was fired on by batteries and riflemen on the Fedioukine Heights, and also by batteries and riflemen on the Northern slope of the Causeway Heights. It then came under the direct fire of twelve guns in its front. A steady gallop was maintained, until what remained of the four squadrons got near the guns, when the pace was increased to an estimated speed of seventeen miles an hour, and our men, galloping through the battery went headlong into the Russian Cavalry which remained at the halt, until the men turned their backs before the handful of British soldiers.

Meanwhile the 4th Regiment Chasseurs d'Afrique, got on the flank of the Russian batteries and so effectively silenced them, that the survivors of the Light brigade were not inconvenienced in their retreat by the fire of guns on that side.

The Heavy brigade was moved forward until it came under effective fire; but eventually, Lord Lucan considering, that the only result of keeping the brigade in this forward position would be to incur useless loss, he retired it; and in fact comparatively little damage was done to the survivors of the Light brigade in their retreat.

The Light brigade charge—albeit the Russian battery was wrecked, the Russian cavalry driven off the field, and the Russian infantry induced to fall back in squares—was nevertheless a glorious failure, since we left the Russians in possession of the three redoubts and our 12-pounder guns. The charge of the Heavy brigade was, on the contrary, an astounding success. But the terrible loss incurred by the Light brigade squadrons, and the glamour thrown over their wild ride by the impressive verses of the Laureate, entirely blinded the Public as to the material military value of the two exploits.

Distance and expense must militate against officers in ordinary circumstances visiting this historical valley, but though the luxuriant grass and wild flowers which adorned it in spring forty years ago have now disappeared, being replaced by cultivation, yet its shape cannot alter, and to the end of Time any one interested in the deeds of our cavalry, when standing on the edge of the Upland, will have no difficulty in tracing the course of those who, it may be truly said, in devoted obedience to orders rushed "to glory or the grave."

1858

A VISIT TO A KALMUCK PRINCE
by Alexandre Dumas

IN THE SPRING of 1858, Alexandre Dumas, the elder, set out for Russia to visit some Russian friends. Already famous as one of France's great novelists and travel writers, he was wined and dined by all and sundry.

Dumas spent nine months traveling up to Finland, across to Moscow, down the Volga to the Caspian Sea and on through Astrakhan to the Caucasus. While he was at Astrakhan, Dumas was invited to visit Prince Toumaine, a Kalmuck prince who lived not far away. The prince arranged a gala feast for his distinguished guest, who enjoyed the colorful festivities with all his usual verve and his unfailing sense of humor.

At eight o'clock on the 29th [September] we embarked in the *Verbliond* and moved slowly upstream against the current, reaching our destination at about half past ten. The left bank of the Volga was crowded with Kalmucks to greet us, the landing stage was gay with flags, and as we hove in sight the prince's artillery saluted us, our boat replying with its two little cannon.

It was easy to distinguish the figure of the prince, waiting for us on the landing stage, wearing national costume—a white coat, very tight and fastened from top to bottom with tiny buttons, a kind of flat Polish *chapska* on his head, loose trousers and boots of Morocco leather. I had taken care to make sure of the correct procedure beforehand, and followed it precisely. Since the feast was being given in my honour, I duly went straight up to the prince, threw my arms around him, and rubbed his nose with mine, a gesture which expresses every good wish. Prince Toumaine was a man of 30 or 32, fairly tall and rather fat, with very small hands and feet. (The average Kalmuck lives in the saddle from early childhood, so his feet do not grow in the usual way. The continual pressure on the stirrup broadens them until they are almost square.)

The castle was 200 yards from the river bank and a guard of honour escorted us to the open front door, where we were received by the major domo. He conducted us through the palace until we reached a closed door on which he gave a ceremonial knock. Instantly it was flung open by some invisible means, and we were in the presence of the Princess of the Kalmucks.

She was seated on a kind of throne. Her maids of honour, six to the right and six to the left, were squatting on their heels, all as motionless as statues in a pagoda. The princess was arrayed in a robe of Persian silk embroidered in gold, open at the front to reveal the bodice of her dress, gleaming with pearls and diamonds. Around her neck she wore a plain linen collar, like a man's, fastened in front with two huge pearls. Her headdress was square, the upper part consisting of ostrich feathers dyed red, the lower part divided and turned back to reveal her brow.

She was not quite twenty, and the Chinese slant of her eyes was vastly becoming; her nose was a fraction less pointed than our European taste would consider perfect, and her red lips were parted over her pearly teeth. (How I wished the ceremonial was the same for women as for men! I should have thoroughly enjoyed rubbing noses with the princess!)

120

The prince asked if we would care to attend a Service to celebrate our visit. He had ordered the High Priest to arrange it with special prayers to the Dalai Lama for our well-being and happiness. We replied that we should be delighted, whereupon the prince added in a conversational aside: "It won't take long. Then we can enjoy a meal."

The assembled company began to move towards the door. At the palace gate two fine carriages were waiting and a score of horses with the traditional Kalmuck saddles raised a foot or so above the animal's spine so that the rider is standing rather than sitting. I was awarded the honour of riding with the princess, my friends entered the second carrriage, and the prince mounted his horse. Scarcely had we taken our seats when, at a word from their mistress, the court ladies instantly relaxed their rigidity, hitched their robes between their legs as high as possible, and, without using the stirrups, leapt astride the first horse they could reach. Then, bare to the knees and shrieking with excitement, their head-dresses slipping this way and that until they looked positively tipsy, they galloped off towards the pagoda a few hundred yards away.

The doors of the pagoda stood wide open, the temple itself silent until the moment when the prince and princess set foot on the threshold. Then there burst forth an incredible din like some cacophony from the underworld. Twenty musicians faced each other across the broad aisle leading to the altar, some beating drums, cymbals, tomtoms, others blowing with distended cheeks into trumpets, conches, or great tubes ten feet long. The greater the noise, the more they are glorifying the Dalai Lama, or so they believe.

On returning to the castle we found the courtyard crowded with Kalmucks, three hundred or more assembled to enjoy the feast that the prince was providing in my honour, for which his servants had slaughtered a horse, two cows and twenty sheep. The choicer portions of horsemeat, minced with onion, pepper and salt, are eaten raw as an appetiser, a national dish, that the prince asked me to taste! Before we sat down ourselves, the prince made sure that his Kalmucks had all that they could want, and, as if he felt the need to apologise for the slight delay, he explained: "Those are the people on whom my way of life depends. It is only right that I should give them a little pleasure on an occasion like this." He is a real humanitarian and very rich, though his wealth lies chiefly in flocks and herds—fifty thousand horses, thirty thousand camels and more sheep than can be counted—eleven or twelve millions.

For his visitors Prince Toumaine had provided the choicest delicacies at his command, meat from a young camel and a six months-old colt, lambs, chickens, game in overwhelming abundance. When at last we reached the dessert stage, the prince asked me to come to the window, glass in hand, to receive a toast from the Kalmucks still feasting outside. As I appeared they all rose to their feet, each with his wooden drinking vessel in one hand and a half-gnawed bone in the other, gave me a cheer and drank my health. The prince decided that my glass was too small for an adequate response, so he handed me a great horn bound with silver, poured into it a whole bottle of champagne, and though I am no drinker I managed to drain it in honour of his subects, the 300 in the courtyard and their 11,000 fellow-serfs throughout his realm.

After that Homeric repast, we all walked across the courtyard between rows of wildly cheering Kalmucks to a dais that had been erected while we feasted.

"Now," said the prince, "you shall see how a Kalmuck moves house."

Four camels, laden with a tent and everything needed by a nomad family, were led forward by the father, mother and two sons. At a word of command, the great creatures kneeled while their loads were removed, then wandered off to graze while their owners erected the *kibitka*. Ten minutes later, everything was in place. One of the sons came to the dais, offering us the hospitality of his father's tent, and soon I was sitting crosslegged on a carpet beside the prince and princess accepting a cup of Kalmuck tea. Full of confidence I raised it to my lips, and instantly felt certain I had been poisoned! It was the most abominable beverage that ever turned a Christian stomach! (I found that it was made from a piece of tea-brick from China, boiled in a saucepan with milk, butter and salt.) Next we were offered fermented mare's milk but this time I was more cautious, and after passing it across my firmly closed mouth, murmuring appreciation to please my host, I placed the glass on the ground and took the first opportunity of upsetting it.

Our visit over, we thanked our host, and returned to our former seats on the dais. The same instant the nomads began to take down their tent, piled their chattels in a pyramid on their camels, seated themselves on the apex of the load, the father on the first, the mother on the second, followed by their sons. They filed before us, crossing their hands on their breasts and bowing, then galloped off, silhouetted for a moment against the skyline before disappearing behind a hillock.

1861

THE SERF'S MIND
by an Anonymous Englishman

THE ANONYMOUS ENGLISHMAN who reports on his conversation with some serfs tells us in the preface to his book by way of credentials that he has "spent fifteen years of a long life among the Russians in active business of divers kinds, by which I have been brought into close contact with men of all grades throughout the empire."

In addition his publishers say that he knows more than most travelers, not only because he lived for many years in the country, but chiefly because he knows "how to observe and seize at once the point of any character or incident."

At the time of the publication of his book, the author was still living in Russia, and it was probably to avoid embarrassment to himself and to his Russian friends that he chose to write anonymously. For at the time he was writing (1861), Alexander II had just emancipated the serfs; and although the act had not yet been put into effect, the whole country realized that it signaled the beginning of an economic revolution. As a result, the atmosphere in Russia was tense.

Before 1863, when the act was to take effect, who could know the results of the emancipation of thirty millions of serfs? While among the peasants, journeying from one part to another, about the time of the first edict on the subject, I tried to ascertain what value the peasants themselves set on the promised boon; but I could not find my way far into the mass of their ignorance and apathy.

One day I had the following conversation with a serf who brought me a message:

"Your name is Evan Vasiliovitch; to whom do you belong?"

"I am the serf of Karmoritch."

"How many are you?"

"Two thousand souls are we."

"You will all soon be free."

He looked at me from the corners of his eyes, and drawled out,

"Yes; if God and our Father wills."

"It will be better for you, Evan; will it not?"

"God knows, baron. How should I know?"

"How much obrok [a yearly tax] do you pay?"

"Thirty roubles a year."

"Do you pay it in work or in money?"

"I work four days a week in the sugar-fabric, to pay the obrok, passport and taxes."

"How much are the passport and taxes?"

"About three roubles and a half, besides other things."

"That is thirty-three roubles and a half you have to pay; and for this you have to work four days every week in the sugar-mill?"

"It is so, baron; and hard work it is."

"When you get your freedom, you will not require to pay obrok, or to work for it. Your time will be your own to cultivate your ground. Will that not be better for you?"

"God give it; I don't know. But I am tired of working."

"How much land have you?"

"Three and a half deciatines" (ten acres).

"Well that is plenty to keep your family on. If you spend all your time on it and pay no obrok, is it not plenty?"

"I don't know, baron; but I am tired of working in the fabric."

"Now tell me, Evan, what do you intend to do when you get your freedom?"

He turned his eyes first up, then down, then on both sides, as if seeking to evade an answer; gave the peculiar peasant's shrug, and slowly muttered,

"I shall sleep, baron."

"And after you have slept, Evan?"

"I shall eat, baron."

"And after you have eaten, Evan?"

"I shall sleep again, baron."

"And when the black bread is gone; and when the pig and poultry are all eaten; and when the potatoes, carrots, and cabbages are all eaten; and when there is no firewood nor pasture,—what will you do then, Evan?"

"Then I will tell you, baron. Now may God give you health; and thank you for the tea-money you are going to give me. Give you good-day!"

I believe this is the case of nearly all the serfs. The condition of many of them at this time may be judged from the following account of himself I got with difficulty from a peasant who worked in a cotton-mill:

"I earn four roubles [about two dollars] a month. My time is all spent in the mill—from five o'clock in the morning until eight o'clock at night. My wife and two daughters work on the fields belonging to the baron five days every week in summer. They get no wages. In winter they do any kind of work required of them by the steward. My son (who is seventeen years old) works also in the mill, and gets two roubles a month. We have three deciatines of land. It is our own; so is the house. We can only raise a few potatoes, cabbages, and carrots. The women do this work. We keep a pig, and we have some ducks. We eat them. We get black bread from the econom (the steward's shop); this is deducted from our wages. We pay no obrok from these wages, no taxes. Our work is counted for this: the steward manages all that. Somehow I am always in debt to the steward's office. I have worked ten years in the mill and am a good spinner. I don't know what we shall do when we get our freedom. We shall not work any more, I suppose. I may go begging; it is an easy life. I am now unfit for outdoor work; but my son is able: let him cultivate the land. We are three thousand souls on this estate. A thousand nearly are away, and pay forty roubles obrok each a year. They pay their own passports and taxes besides."

This is a sorry but true picture. Eleven pounds a year had this man and his family to live on! For this sum the father and son gave all their time in the mill, and the mother and two daughters five days a week in other work. In a free mill worked on the free principle, the father and son alone would be worth, and sure to receive, about sixty pounds, and the two daughters thirty; but then they could be forced to pay out of that what their master chose to exact for obrok and taxes. Many of the serfs are better off, and some are worse. The serfs belonging at one time to the crown are now free; and those possessed by the rich old families have paid five roubles obrok, and done what they pleased with their ground or themselves. Some of them are immensely rich, and could purchase their freedom at fabulous sums; but great nobles sometimes choose to retain them, either as a reserve-fund in case of need, or from a foolish vanity in the possession of a serf worth half a million roubles. Such instances, however, are by no means common.

1865

A RUSSIAN HOME
by Theophile Gautier

THEOPHILE GAUTIER (1811–1872), the well-known French writer, paid a visit to Russia in 1866. A man of a kindly and exceptionally charming nature, he was widely entertained during his stay. An experienced traveler, he proved to be a discerning observer whose report on the Russian scene is outstanding both because of its content and because of the grace and verve of his writing.

An ante-chamber in Russia is not like such a room in any other quarter of the world. The pelisses hung on the rack, with their sleeves and broad pleats, look something like human figures suspended there. The galoches underneath simulate feet, so that the effect of all these furs in the dim light is indeed strange.

A Russian apartment unites with comfort all the luxury of English and French civilization. At first sight one could fancy himself in

London or Paris, but soon the local character betrays itself in a thousand minute details. First of all the Byzantine Madonna, with her child, surrounded with carvings of silver or enamel, illumined by the flame of a lamp that is never extinguished, makes you realize that you are neither in London nor Paris, but in orthodox, Holy Russia. Sometimes the image of the Saviour replaces that of the Virgin.

Then the climate demands certain requirements that cannot be ignored. Everywhere the windows are double and the space between them is filled with sand, which is often covered with moss. On account of the double sashes, the windows in Russia have neither shutters nor blinds, they can neither be opened nor shut, for the sashes are fixed for the entire winter, and are carefully fastened. A narrow casement serves to renew the air, a disagreeable and even dangerous operation, on account of the great difference between the indoor and exterior temperature. Thick curtains of rich stuffs deaden the feeling of any cold that might come through the glass. The rooms are larger and higher than in Paris. Since all the rooms are hermetically sealed and the halls heated, the temperature is sixty-six to sixty-eight degrees, which allows the women to wear muslins and have their arms and neck bare. The furnaces emit heat at night as well as during the day. Hot steam pipes or great stoves of monumental proportions, of fine white or painted porcelain, and reaching to the ceiling, scatter heat where the furnaces cannot reach!

Flowers are indeed a truly Russian luxury. The houses overflow with them! Flowers receive you at the door and mount the stairs with you. Irish ivy festoons the balustrade, jardinieres are on every landing. In the embrasure of the windows are tall banana trees; talipots, magnolias, camellias in flower reach to the gilded ceilings, orchids hang suspended from glass, china, or terra-cotta pockets. Pieces of Japanese or Bohemian glassware in the center of the tables or the corners of the sideboards overflow with the exotic blossoms. In the streets you are at the arctic pole, but in the house you could fancy yourself in the tropics.

It is as though by this profusion of bloom the eye were seeking to console itself for the interminable whiteness of the winter. The longing to see something that is not white must become a sort of agony in a land where the earth is covered with snow for more than six months of the year.

As for the furniture, it is like ours, only larger, more ample, as it must be, in view of the dimensions of the room. But it is the cabinet that is entirely Russian. It is made from a delicate precious wood, carved in openwork like the sticks of a fan, and occupies a corner of the drawing-room and is festooned with rare running plants. It is a sort of confessional for intimate conversations, furnished inside with divans, where the mistress of the house can isolate herself from the mass of her guests, and at the same time remaining with them can receive three or four guests of distinction. Sometimes the cabinet is in colored glass, flowered with pictures, and mounted in panels of gilded leather. Nor is it at all unusual to see, amid the ottomans, easy chairs, a gigantic white bear, stuffed and padded like a sofa and offering to visitors an altogether arctic seat. Little black bears often serve as stools.

The bed-chamber is not generally furnished with the luxury and elegance given to it in France. Behind a screen or carved partition, a little, low bed is tucked away, like a camp-bed or divan. The Russians are of Eastern origin, and even in the upper classes they do not care for the sweetness of a comfortable couch. They sleep anywhere they may happen to be, like the Turks, often in their pelisses, on the broad, green leather sofas, that are in every corner. The ancient habits of the tent seem to have followed them into the very heart of that civilization, with whose every elegance and every vice they are acquainted.

Rich hangings adorn the walls, and should the master of the

129

house pride himself on his artistic tastes, there will certainly be crimson damask from India, or dark embroidered stuffs, or, surrounded by rich frames, a Horace Vernet, a Gudin, or, if he desire to prove his patriotism, a Bruloff and an Aïvasovsky—who are the most fashionable painters.

The interior we have just described is not that of a palace, but of a house, not of the middle class,—this word means nothing in Russia—but of a house that is *comme il faut*.

1867

WE ARE RECEIVED BY THE EMPEROR OF RUSSIA
by Mark Twain

IN 1867 Mark Twain, already successful as a journalist, a lecturer and the author of the popular "The Celebrated Jumping Frog of Calaveras County," persuaded a San Francisco newspaper, the *Daily Alta,* to send him as its correspondent with a group of "distinguished people" who had chartered the steamship *Quaker City* to take them on a tour of the Mediterranean and the Holy Land. The *Quaker City,* ancestor of today's popular cruise ships, made a stop at Yalta to give its load of American tourists an opportunity of an audience with Tsar Alexander II. Mark Twain took the occasion in his stride, observing everything with a reporter's detachment and the irrepressible humor which was his trademark. The travel letters which Mark Twain sent home to his newspaper at each port of call later formed the nucleus of his famous travel book, *Innocents Abroad.*

We anchored here at Yalta, Russia, two or three days ago. To me the place was a vision of the Sierras. The tall, gray mountains that back it, their sides bristling with pines—cloven with ravines—here and

there a hoary rock towering into view—long, straight, streaks sweep-
ing down from the summit to the sea, marking the passage of some
avalanche of former times—all these were as like what one sees in the
Sierras as if the one were a portrait of the other. The little village of
Yalta nestles at the foot of an amphitheatre which slopes backward
and upward to the wall of hills, and looks as if it might have sunk
quietly down to its present position from a higher elevation. This
depression is covered with the great parks and gardens of noblemen,
and through the mass of green foliage the bright colors of their
palaces bud out here and there like flowers. It is a beautiful spot.

At the appointed hour we drove out three miles, and assembled
in the handsome garden in front of the Emperor's palace.

We formed a circle under the trees before the door, for there
was no one room in the house able to accommodate our three score
persons comfortably, and in a few minutes the imperial family came
out bowing and smiling, and stood in our midst. A number of
great dignitaries of the empire, in undress uniforms, came with
them. With every bow, His Majesty said a word of welcome. I copy
these speeches. There is character in them—Russian character—which
is politeness itself, and the genuine article. The French are polite,
but it is often mere ceremonious politeness. A Russian imbues his
polite things with a heartiness, both of phrase and expression, that
compels belief in their sincerity. As I was saying, the Tsar punctuated
his speeches with bows:

"Good morning—I am glad to see you—I am gratified—I am
delighted—I am happy to receive you!"

All took off their hats and the consul inflicted the address [writ-
ten by Mark Twain] on him. He bore it with unflinching fortitude;
then took the rusty-looking document and handed it to some great
officer or other, to be filed away among the archives of Russia—in the
stove. He thanked us for the address, and said he was very much
pleased to see us, especially as such friendly relations existed between

Russia and the United States. The Empress said the Americans were favorites in Russia, and she hoped the Russians were similarly regarded in America. These were all the speeches that were made, and I recommend them to parties who present policemen with gold watches, as models of brevity and point. After this the Empress went and talked sociably (for an Empress) with various ladies around the circle; several gentlemen entered into a disjointed general conversation with the Emperor; the Dukes and Princes, Admirals and Maids of Honor dropped into free-and-easy chat with first one and then another of our party, and whoever chose stepped forward and spoke with the modest little Grand Duchess Marie, the Tsar's daughter. She is fourteen years old, light-haired, blue-eyed, unassuming, and pretty. Everybody talks English.

The Emperor wore a cap, frock-coat and pantaloons, all of some kind of plain white drilling—cotton or linen—and sported no jewelry or any insignia whatever of rank. No costume could be less ostentatious. He is very tall and spare, and a determined-looking man, though a very pleasant-looking one, nevertheless. It is easy to see that he is kind and affectionate. There is something very noble in his expression when his cap is off. There is none of that cunning in his eyes that all of us noticed in Louis Napoleon's.

It seemed strange—stranger than I can tell—to think that the central figure in the cluster of men and women, chatting here under the trees like the most ordinary individual in the land, was a man who could open his lips and ships would fly through the waves, locomotives would speed over the plains, couriers would hurry from village to village, a hundred telegraphs would flash the word to the four corners of an empire that stretches its vast proportions over a seventh part of the habitable globe, and a countless multitude of men would spring to do his bidding. I had a sort of vague desire to examine his hands and see if they were of flesh and blood, like other men's. Here was a man who could do this wonderful thing, and yet if I chose I could knock him down. If he were grievously ill, all the nations would know it before the sun rose again; if he dropped lifeless where he stood, his fall might shake the thrones of half a world! If I could have stolen his coat, I would have done it. When I meet a man like that, I want something to remember him by.

As a general thing we have been shown through palaces by some plush-legged, filigreed flunkey or other, who charged a franc for it; but after talking with the company half an hour, the Emperor of Russia and his family conducted us all through their mansion themselves. They made no charge. They seemed to take a real pleasure in it.

We spent half an hour idling through the palace, admiring the cosy apartments and the rich but eminently home-like appointments of the place, and then the imperial party bade our party a kind goodbye, and proceeded to count the spoons.

1872–1874

THE CIRCLE OF TCHAYKÓVSKY
by P. Kropotkin

Born into an aristocratic Moscow family that traced its descent back to the Grand Princes of Smolensk, educated at the school for pages, an institution that was attached to the imperial household, and already distinguished as a scientist, Peter Kropotkin at the age of thirty gave up a brilliant career in science to become a revolutionary. Like Tolstoy, Kropotkin was an idealist and a reformer to whom the condition of his fellow man was of paramount importance. To help that common man to escape from an economic des-

133

potism and achieve his individual freedom seemed to him to be the most important work a man could do.

In the Russia of the 1870s, there was a great surge of revolutionary activity. Alexander II's reign, which had started out with so much promise, had turned into a regime of reaction and terror. The freeing of the serfs, which in 1861 had seemed to herald a better era, had been so hedged in by compromise and unworkable restrictions that it left the peasants worse off than before. The social movement, however, was gaining momentum, and Kropotkin joined one of the "circles" that were mushrooming all over the country. Once a member of a socialist group, his life followed a cycle that was characteristic for a man of Kropotkin's conviction in the Russia of that time: he was arrested, he was sent to prison, and he was exiled.

Soon after my return [to St. Petersburg] Kelnitz invited me to join a circle which was known amongst the youth as "the Circle of Tchaykóvsky." Under this name it played an important part in the history of the social movement in Russia. "Its members," Kelnitz said to me, "have hitherto been mostly constitutionalists; but they are excellent men, with minds open to an honest idea; they have plenty of friends all over Russia, and you will see later on what they can do."

The beginning of this circle was a very small group of young men and women who had united for the purposes of self-education and self-improvement. In 1869 Necháieff had tried to start a secret revolutionary organization among the youth imbued with the desire of working among the people, and to secure this end he resorted to the ways of old conspirators, without recoiling even before deceit when he wanted to force his associates to follow his lead. Such methods could have no success in Russia, and very soon his society broke down. All the members were arrested, and some of the best and purest of the Russian youth went to Siberia before they had done anything. The circle of self-education of which I am speaking was constituted in opposition to the methods of Necháieff. The few friends had judged, quite correctly, that a morally developed in-

134

dividuality must be the foundation of every organization, whatever political character it may take afterward, and whatever programme of action it may adopt in the course of future events.

At that time, however—that is, in 1872—the circle had nothing revolutionary in it. But the members found a suitable work. They began to spread good books and distributed them among students in the provinces. In a few years there was not a town of importance where this circle did not have a group of comrades engaged in the spreading of that sort of literature [on history, condition of the laboring classes, etc.]. Gradually, the circle became more and more a center of socialistic propaganda among the educated youth, and a natural intermediary between members of provincial circles; and then, one day, the ice between students and workers was broken, and direct relations were established with working-people at St. Petersburg and in some of the provinces.

When I joined the Circle of Tchaykóvsky, I found its members hotly discussing the direction to be given to their activity. Some were in favour of continuing to carry on radical and socialistic propaganda among the educated youth; but others thought that the sole aim of this work should be to prepare men who would be capable of arousing the great inert labour masses, and that their chief activity ought to be among the peasants and workmen in the towns.

We often spoke, of course, of the necessity of a political agitation against our absolute government. We saw already that the mass of the peasants were being driven to unavoidable and irremediable ruin by foolish taxation, and by still more foolish selling off of their cattle to cover the arrears of taxes. We "visionaries" saw coming the complete ruin of a whole population. We knew, and we learned more every day, of the lawlessness of the functionaries, and the almost incredible bestiality of many among them. We heard continually of friends whose houses were raided at night by the police, who disappeared in prisons, and who—we ascertained later on—had been transported without judgment to hamlets in some remote province of Russia. We felt, therefore, the necessity of a political struggle against this terrible power, which was crushing the best intellectual forces of a nation.

The two years that I worked with the Circle of Tchaykóvsky, before I was arrested, left a deep impression upon all my subsequent life and thought. During these two years it was life under high pressure I was in a family of men and women so closely united by their common object, and so broadly and delicately humane in their mutual relations, that I cannot even now recall a single moment of even temporary friction marring the life of our circle.

My sympathies went especially toward the weavers and the workers of the cotton factories. There are many thousands of them at St. Petersburg, who work there during the winter, and return for the three summer months to their native villages to cultivate the land. Half peasants and half town workers, they had generally retained the social spirit of the Russian villager. The movement spread like wildfire among them. Most of them lived in small associations or *artéls,* ten or twelve persons hiring a common apartment and taking their meals together, each one paying every month his share of the general expenses. It was to these lodgings that we used to go, and the weavers brought us into contact with other artéls, of stonemasons, carpenters and the like. Besides, we had in different parts of St. Petersburg special apartments, kept by some of our people, to which ten or twelve workers would come every night, to learn reading and writing, and after that to have a talk. From time to time one of us went to the native villages of our town friends, and spent a couple of weeks in almost open propaganda amongst the peasants.

Amongst [the workers] I spent my happiest hours. New Year's Day of 1874, the last I spent in Russia at liberty, is especially memorable to me. The previous evening I had been in a choice company. Inspiring, noble words were spoken that night about the citizen's duties, the well-being of the country and the like. But underneath all the thrilling speeches one note sounded: How could each of the speakers preserve his own personal well-being? I returned home seized suddenly with profound sadness amid all this talk.

Next morning I went to one of our weavers' meetings. It took place in an underground dark room. I was dressed as a peasant, and was lost in the crowd of other sheepskins. My comrade, who was known to the workers, simply introduced me: "A friend." "Tell us," he said, "what you have seen abroad."

The audience consisted mostly of middle-aged people. They were intensely interested. They asked me questions, all to the point about the minute details of the working-men's unions, the aims of the International Association and its chances of success. And then came questions about what could be done in Russia and the prospects of our propaganda. I never minimized the dangers of our agitation, and frankly said what I thought. *"We* shall probably be sent to Siberia, one of these days; and you—part of you—will be kept long months in prison for having listened to us." This gloomy prospect did not frighten them. "After all, there are men in Siberia, too—not bears only." "Where men are living others can live." "The devil is not so terrible as they paint him." "If you are afraid of wolves, never go into the wood," they said, as we parted. And when, afterward, several of them were arrested, they nearly all behaved bravely, sheltering us and betraying no one.

1876

A LETTER TO FLAUBERT
by Turgenev

DURING TURGENEV's last years in France, he made many friends in the French literary world. A favorite among them was Gustave Flaubert, the author of *Madame Bovary*.

On the death of his mother in 1850, Turgenev had inherited the family estate in the town of Mtsensk, province of Orel, where he at once freed the serfs. In the letter that follows, the Squire of Mtsensk, back home on a visit, describes Russian country life to the Squire of Croisset.

> Spasskoïé, Province of Orel,
> Town of Mtsensk
> Tuesday, June 23—July 4, 1876

My dear old Boy,—I'm writing to you from here to Croisset—from one Patmos to another. Your letter reached me yesterday, and, as you see, I have not delayed in answering it.

So you're working at Croisset. Well, now I'm going to astonish you! Never in my life have I worked as I've been working here. I spend sleepless nights, bent double over my writing table. I'm once more filled with the illusion that I can say, not exactly something different from what has ever been said before—that I don't care about—but that I can say it differently. And note that, besides this, I'm overwhelmed with miscellaneous work—with money affairs, "administrative and farming business," and Heaven knows what!

You want to know what my abode looks like. It is a wooden house, very old, faced with beams, and distempered a pale lilac. There is a verandah in front, covered with creeping ivy; the two roofs are made of iron and painted green. This little house is all that remains of a vast horseshoe shaped building which was burnt down in 1870.

Yesterday evening with your letter in my pocket, I sat myself down on my venerable steps facing about sixty peasant women, almost all dressed in red and very ugly (with one exception, in the shape of a newly-married girl of sixteen, who had just had fever, and was astonishingly like the Sistine Madonna at Dresden). They danced like marmosettes, or rather like bears, and sang with very harsh and hard but true voices. It was a little fête they had asked me to get up, and a very simple matter it was—two buckets of brandy, some cakes and some nuts, and there you are! They kept preening themselves for my benefit, and I watched them doing it and felt horribly sad. The little Sistine Madonna is called Mary, as is fitting.

Enough of this. I will write you again before leaving here. Meanwhile I send you my best love.

Your old friend,
Iv. Turgenev

P.S.—I find that in point of colouring the whole landscape is pale here—sky, vegetation, soil—rather a warm, golden paleness. It would be merely pretty but for its big outlines and great level spaces, which lend it grandeur.

OUR LIFE IN KARA PRISON
by Leo Deutsch

BEGINNING with the latter half of the sixteenth century, when Russia was first consolidated under the tsars, all manifestations of free thought were suppressed by a succession of autocratic governments. An underground movement, secret societies and increasingly daring subversive activities became more and more common. In 1863, sparked by the Polish revolt, the reform movement sponsored by the intelligentsia of the upper and middle classes took on the character of what can only be called a revolutionary movement. The Russian government responded to this by treating the offenders with increased severity, and more and more citizens were exiled to Siberia—generally without the formalities of a trial. The usual routine was first the prison term, then the work camp and finally release under police supervision.

Leo Deutsch, the author of the pages that follow, was a leader in the revolutionary movement and one of the founders of the Social Democratic Labor Party. Arrested for smuggling socialistic literature from Switzerland into Russia, he was sentenced to thirteen years and four months in prison and lifetime banishment. He served his prison term at Kara, one of the most notorious of the Siberian prisons for male "politicals." Released "under surveillance," he succeeded in making his escape.

On my arrival at the Kara prison I found in existence there an extremely elaborate organisation regulating the prisoner's daily life, a system that the course of time had evolved and tested. The fundamental principle of the arrangement was equality of rights and duties; the inmates of the prison forming for all domestic purposes a commune or *artél*. It was free to anyone to enter this *artél* or to remain outside, and whichever they did, material conditions—in the way of food, etc.—were the same for all. The Government provided a certain quantity of food per day for each prisoner—about 3¼lbs.

of bread, nearly 6 oz. of meat, a few ounces of meal, and some salt. Friends of prisoners were permitted to furnish them with the means of obtaining extra provisions, and some of us, received such contributions regularly, this money as well as the government allowances becoming the common property of the *artél*. The money was distributed as follows: part was set aside to supplement the food rations, especially for buying more meat (this was called in our lingo "provisioning the stock-pot"); another portion was reserved for what was called common expenses—assistance to those who were leaving the prison and going to their appointed place of exile, subscriptions to such newspapers as we were allowed, postage, etc.; and a third part was divided equally among all for pocket-money.

Every morning the *staròsta* [the elected leader] presented himself with his order-book at the doors of the different rooms, and asked what was wanted. One would order a "sou's" worth of sugar, another a "brick" of tea and so on. These orders were entered, to be later transferred to the account-book, and soon afterwards the *staròsta* would bring the articles and give them to us through the peephole. The *staròsta* also received from the steward for distribution all things that were due us in the way of clothing, linen, and so forth, and he was our representative in all our dealings with the commandant. The election of the *staròsta* was by ballot, and for a term of six months.

All work within the prison precincts we shared amongst us; but such services as made it necessary to go outside the yard (carrying wood and water, etc.) were performed by ordinary criminals whom we tipped. Our own duties were of two kinds: work for the community—such as cooking, cleaning the rooms, attending to the steam baths; and private work—washing clothes, mending, etc. Everyone except the weak or ill had to take his share in the former. The cooking was undertaken by groups of five men, each group serving for a week at a time. Each group had its head cook, his assistant, a cook for the invalids, and two helpers. The work was not light and was in no way attractive; it began between six and seven in the morning, and was not over before five in the evening, by which hour one would be thoroughly tired out. On the other hand, the labour was a welcome relief to the monotony of our lives, and the kitchen was a meeting place for the inhabitants of different rooms, forming a sort of club-house for those engaged in the cooking.

Our cooks had to manage with very scanty materials. Our culinary skill was chiefly displayed in the way of serving up the soup-meat at a subsequent meal. The dish most favoured by the majority was meat cut into small pieces and mixed with groats; this was called "Everyone-likes-it." The cooks generally put their best foot forward on Saturday, when their week of office expired. For years it had been the custom to have an extra dish on that day, a *piròg*, or sort of pie made of flour, rice, and mince. The cooks used to save up scraps of meat for it all through the week.

Besides the head-man who had charge of our larder, a special "bread-dispenser" was appointed, whose office it was to cut up the loaves and divide them amongst the different rooms; he had also to collect all scraps and crumbs that were left, and send them on to our comrades in the penal settlement, where they were used to feed a horse and a couple of cows belonging to the *artél*.

The "poultry-keeper" was another of our officials. We kept in the yard a number of fowls which we cherished most carefully, and they were a great amusement to us.

Two other comrades were "bath-keepers"; had to see to the cleaning of the steam-bath, etc.,—and—like all our "officials"—were excused from kitchen work.

Finally there was the very important post of librarian, which ranked next to that of *staròsta,* and, like it, was decided by ballot. In the course of years our library had attained quite imposing dimensions; it was composed partly of books brought by the inmates, partly of those sent to us as gifts. Nearly all branches of knowledge were represented in it, particularly history, mathematics, and natural sciences; there were also books in almost every European language, including the classics. Two enormous cupboards in the corridor contained this treasure, but the greater part of it was usually in the hands of eager readers.

In the middle of each room hung a lamp with a dark shade—lamps that we had ourselves provided. Our table was narrow and long, so that a number of persons necessarily sat where the light was very poor, insufficient for work of any kind; and this, of course, was a misfortune for everyone, as those condemned to idleness disturbed the more advantageously placed, who wanted to study. Anyone who was really bent on earnest study had to devise a special plan: he became what we called a "Sirius." This meant that as soon as it became dusk he went to bed till midnight, and then, while the rest were asleep, got up and worked till dawn, when Sirius rises above the horizon; after which he lay down for another two hours' rest. It needed an overwhelming desire for learning and considerable powers of endurance to become a "Sirius"; it was difficult to rest when the comrades were chattering and making a noise all around one, and when one had at last managed to get off to sleep, it seemed immediately time to wake up again. Yet there were some amongst us—though not many—who were numbered among the "Siriuses" all the time I was at Kara.

That our life must have had much in it irksome in the extreme and hard to bear is only too evident; living in such constant and close intimacy for years with the same set of people must necessarily lead to all kinds of petty rubs and differences; all the more because the forced inactivity was such a strain on the nerves of many. These were evils not in our power entirely to avert.

1880–1881

THE NIHILISTS
by the Dowager Marchioness of Dufferin and Ava

IN 1878, the Marquis of Dufferin and Ava was appointed British Ambassador to Russia. In February 1879, he and his wife arrived in Moscow where, as Lady Dufferin at once noted, "a dark cloud of anarchism hung over the chief cities, unrest and discontent were spoken of on all sides." In less than two years Lady Dufferin's worst fears were realized, and Alexander II was assassinated. The ironic fact was that, as tsars go, Alexander was a liberal ruler. His reign began with a series of reforms which unfortunately pleased neither the liberals nor the reactionaries because Alexander's desire for a modern state was contradicted by his devotion to the "Old Russia." Although he liberated the serfs, the freedom they gained was in many cases less bearable than the old servitude where they were at least protected by their "lords." The landowners, on the other hand, felt they had been badly treated, and the liberal intelligentsia, who championed the peasants, were disillusioned by the slow pace at which Alexander was leading the advance to the modern state. They became increasingly restive and as a result they were met by stricter police supervision and stricter censorship. Convinced that only a campaign of terror would produce results, they assassinated the Tsar in 1881. The murder gained them little, for the comparatively liberal Alexander was succeeded by the autocratic and reactionary Alexander III.

Tuesday, February 17.—We dined at the Chanzys', and the evening became historic.

M. de Giers [the Foreign Minister] heard a noise before leaving his house, and though he seems to have thought it was at the Palace, he did not go himself, but sent his servant. During dinner a message came to say there had been an explosion "of gas" in the Winter Palace, and before we left in the evening, the report reached us that thirty people were killed. We hurried home, and found Captain

144

Haig in our house. He told us that he was just going to dress for dinner, when he saw a flash of light and his window was blown in: he looked out and found all the passages dark and full of smoke. He got a light and went to see what had happened. The explosion took place two stories below the Emperor's dining-room and was arranged to take place during his dinner. However, the Prince of Hesse was late, and instead of being at table the Emperor and his guests were in the outer room. There was not sufficient damage done in the Emperor's room to have hurt him had he been there, but the windows were all broken. In the room beneath this the guard was dining, and, as far as they knew last night, six men were killed and nineteen were severely wounded.

We hear five carpenters who lived underneath have been taken, and that one escaped. Had the wretches succeeded in their designs they would have killed the Emperor and all his sons, our Duchess [of Edinburgh], and the Prince of Bulgaria and Prince of Hesse.

Wednesday, 18th.—I went to see various people. All are much agitated, and there is a feeling of horror everywhere, especially as it is thought that more efforts will be made before the 19th, the Nihilists having always stated that they would kill the Emperor before that date, the twenty-fifth anniversary of his reign.

Yesterday the Nihilists got out a sheet in which, after first of all avowing that they ordered the explosion, and that a few days ago they had murdered a spy, they advise all persons valuing their lives to keep as far as possible from the Emperor!

A despotic dictator has been appointed. He has power of life and death in his hand, but whether it is a step in the right direction, or whether he can do any good, is a doubtful question.

Sunday, 13th [March, 1881].—We went to church in the morning, but D. [the Marquis of Dufferin and Ava] went to a *manège* where the Ambassadors have an occasional chance of seeing the Emperor. D. had just come in and taken off his uniform when I went out with the two girls to visit a sick woman. She lives quite near us, and on the way we saw a wretched horse with a broken leg being dragged along by soldiers.

When we got into the house the poor woman who was in tears, said to me, "Is it true?" "What?" "Why, that there has been an attempt on the Emperor, and that, if not killed, he is wounded." Then she told me she heard two explosions, and that he was certainly wounded. I almost ran the whole way home to tell D. and at the door I met the secretaries coming with the news,—and then one of the Chancery men told us that he heard the bombs, and then saw the Emperor's carriage with the back and side blown out. D. went off to the Palace, and I have just seen Mr. Kennedy, who went with him and who has left him there. He says a shell was thrown under the Emperor's carriage, which destroyed it but did not wound him; he got out, and another was thrown, wounding him seriously—and they fear he will die. I cannot tell you what a fearful impression it makes upon me, such cruel, persistent murder.

The wretched horse we saw was one ridden by a Cossack close to the carriage,—for you know, since these attempts, the Emperor is always surrounded by mounted soldiers.

4.30.—It is all over. He is dead. D. has not returned yet, but one of the Court officials has brought word. He was insensible when D. arrived there.

Monday, 14th.—The whole story is this. After the parade, the Emperor went and breakfasted with the Grand Duchess Catherine, and on his way back a bomb was thrown at his carriage, which killed a Cossack, wounded some people and horses, and smashed his carriage, which, however, could have taken him home. Instead of driving on, he got out, crossing himself as he did so, and looked around. A second bomb was thrown at his feet and exploded. He was picked up insensible, and taken home in the carriage of the Police Officer, who was also wounded. He died in two hours.

This morning there is a proclamation from the new Emperor—Alexander III.

The Russians go to the Palace to congratulate the new Emperor. "Le roi est mort, vive le roi!"

In the afternoon I went to see my friends the Schouvaloffs. He had been to Court in the morning and said it was a most painful ceremony; every one dressed as for a great fête, but all crying. The new Emperor and Empress terribly overcome. They say she cries all the time, even in the carriage, driving along, when he had to keep acknowledging the salutations of the people. The young Cesarevitch, too, cried during all the service.

Thursday, 17th.—One does nothing but listen to gloomy forebodings and stories of the "incapacity of the police," and the "inefficiency of everybody." The mine now found in a street through which the Emperor might have returned is an immense affair, and, had it been sprung, houses and hundreds of people would have been destroyed. It appears this very place was marked as a suitable spot for a mine, on a map which the Government got last year. The people living in the house were under suspicion, and the house was visited a fortnight ago, but nothing was found.

1886

A COURT BALL
by Mrs. George Van Ness Lothrop

IN THE SPRING of 1885, President Grover Cleveland appointed George Van Ness Lothrop, of Detroit, to the post of Minister Plenipotentiary and Envoy Extraordinary to Russia. Mrs. Lothrop and her three daughters accompanied him to his post. Kindly and sympathetic, human and informal, Mrs. Lothrop wrote home frequently, giving her relatives and friends spirited reports on what may be called the lighter side of diplomatic life.

February 6th, 1886.

The great event of the past week was the first court ball, which was attended by more than two thousand persons. The invitations were for nine o'clock, so we made an effort to be at the Winter Palace at that hour. We went up the stairs and through the halls, watched by hosts of servants in imperial liveries, soldiers with drawn swords, standing like statues, groups of officers and officials, and gaily dressed women. After passing through some splendid rooms, we came to the ball room, in one corner of which was the place appointed for the diplomatic corps. It is a long room and was decorated with fine plants, and lighted by electricity. The incandescent light has just been put in and adapted to the enormous chandeliers, the prisms of which sparkled like diamonds. The light was very steady and becoming, and did not make people look ghastly. Opposite us, leaving a lane between, were Russian ladies, the first in the Empire. They were of course handsomely dressed, and all had fine jewels, which made the group very brilliant. The officers, officials and diplomats, except our own, were all in uniform. The costumes were very handsome, stiff with gold embroidery, and all, I think, wore decorations, some were covered with them,—broad ribbons and insignia of the orders, with jewels. After looking about, talking to the people whom we knew, there was a murmur of expectation, and every one seemed to know that the Emperor and Empress were coming. I have come to the conclusion that their majesties are to the people here what the sun is to the world; I do not expect you to understand it—it must be seen and felt.

When the great doors near us were thrown open the high officials came, then the Grand Master of Ceremonies, then the grand mistress of the Empress' household; after them the Emperor with the Empress on his arm; following them some great officials of the household and the pages, then the Tsarevitch [afterwards Nicholas the Second] with the grand duchess Serge, then a number of grand dukes and grand duchesses, princes etc. The orchestra played a polonaise and they made the tour of the hall. Returning, they formed again. The Empress danced with her son, and the Emperor took the wife of the French Ambassador who, in the absence of Madame Schweinitz [wife of the German Ambassador] is the first lady in the diplomatic corps. Then there were some quadrilles or contre dances after which the Empress went in the next room, where several people were presented to her, and the Emperor walked about saying a few words to different persons. He asked your father to present him to me, and I had the honour of a few words.

The Emperor is a tall, large man, with an air of majesty and command. He does not look sad, nor afraid, nor overwhelmed by the cares and grandness of his position. I do not at all believe he lives in a state of alarm—people say he does not know the sensation of fear. It was most interesting to me to see the man who is ruler over one sixth of the globe, and whose will is law. He wore the uniform of a smart regiment, the Chevaliers Gardes, a red coat and dark trousers, and carried a brass helmet with an eagle on top. He had the blue ribbon of St. Andrew and, I think, its jewelled collar, with many decorations. The Empress was lovely, as she always is. She wore a white dress, not with a long train, a gauze with silver stripes. She had the broad blue ribbon of St. Andrew. She is the only lady who has it; it was given at her coronation. Her dress was low in the neck, and she wore what seemed to be strings of enormous diamonds with great diamonds in her ears. She had several brooches around about the top of her dress, one a diamond so enormous it did not look especially handsome, and a tiara of superb diamonds. She looks so young it is hard to think she is the mother of five children, the oldest seventeen years and more of age. Her figure is as slender and as pretty as that of a young girl; she is altogether charming. The Tsarevitch looks like her, and is very small for a boy of his age. It will be a great misfortune for him if he should not grow. [He never did.] The men of the Imperial family are such large, tall, fine-looking men that the Russians will find it difficult to connect the idea of majesty with one who is so small.

The hall where we had supper was high and large; a balcony ran all around it, and at each end were projecting balconies where two orchestras played alternately. Two thousand people were seated at supper, and served at the same time with no confusion; the supper was excellent. In the middle of the room, but at one side, was the imperial table, where their majesties, the imperial family and the ambassadors and their wives sat. At their right was the table for the diplomatic corps. On the tables, in a line, were arranged great pieces of silver, a design of horses, or of knights, perhaps three feet long, then a silver vase with palms and flowers, then another design, then a silver candelabrum holding fifteen candles, then another fine piece, all of pure silver and close together. If you will try to think how many it would take for two thousand people, it will give you an idea of the silver in the palace. For every two people there was a salt cellar in silver of different shapes. Mine was a bear; on each side were two receptacles, one for salt and one for pepper. The forks, knifes and spoons were all very handsome, many of them were of silver gilt. The china too was very fine. I never saw such wide tables; it seems to me they were more than six feet in width.

They give people much to eat: in one fine room in the center was an immense round table, and a buffet ran all around for tea, cakes, etc. Another buffet, in a corridor, must have been 150 to 200 feet long. At all there were champagne, tea, lemonade, (or what they call such), cakes, ices,—all very handsome. During the evening, ices, the shape and color of fruits were handed around. After the supper, all went to the ballroom, where a waltz was danced that lasted some time; then about one o'clock their majesties left, and the company dispersed.

1890

DEPORTATION BY ÉTAPE
by George Kennan

GEORGE KENNAN (1845–1924) was an American journalist, author and explorer. Due to his lawyer-father's interest in Morse's development of electric telegraph, George Kennan, while still a boy, became an expert telegrapher. Because of this proficiency, he was selected when only twenty years old to go to Siberia as a member of an expedition which the Western Union Telegraph Company was sponsoring to survey a new route for the extension of the telegraphy system from America to Europe via Alaska, Bering Strait and Siberia. Kennan stayed in Siberia two years during which he acquired what proved to be a lifelong interest in the country.

In 1885, Kennan was commissioned by Roswell Smith, president of the Century Company, publishers, to go to Siberia and investigate the prison system. Kennan accepted the commission. At the time he was somewhat prejudiced in favor of the Tsar's government and was not in sympathy with the revolutionists. But after a year of on-the-spot contact with the exiles and a firsthand encounter with the Russian penal system, his sympathies shifted.

Kennan's book, *Siberia and the Exile System,* was the first account of the prisons by a non-Russian to reach the outside world. It caused a sensation, and it is still considered authoritative.

In Tomsk, we had for the first time a satisfactory opportunity to study the life of the Siberian exiles on the road. Marching parties of convicts three or four hundred strong leave Tomsk for Irkútsk weekly throughout the whole year, and make the journey of 1040 miles in about three months. *Étapes,* or exile station-houses, stand along the road at intervals of from twenty-five to forty miles. As the distance from one *étape* to another is too great to be walked in a single day by prisoners in leg-fetters, buildings known as "half-étapes," have been constructed mid-way between the true *étapes* for the shelter of the convicts at night. Marching parties are expected to make about 330 miles a month, with twenty-four hours of rest every third day. Each prisoner receives five cents a day in money for his subsistence, and buys food for himself from peasants along the road who make a business of furnishing it. The dress of the exiles in summer consists of a shirt and a pair of trousers of coarse gray linen; square foot-wrappers of the same material in lieu of stockings; low shoes or slippers; leather ankle-guards to prevent the leg-fetters from chafing; a visorless Glengarry cap; and a long gray overcoat. The dress of female convicts is the same, except that a petticoat takes the place of trousers. Women and children who voluntarily accompany relatives to Siberia are permitted to wear their own clothing, and to carry severally as much baggage as can be put into a two-bushel bag. No distinction is made between common convicts and political convicts, except that the latter, if they are nobles or belong to one of the privileged classes, receive seven and a half cents a day for their subsistence instead of five, and are carried in telégas [small one-horse carts without springs] instead of being forced to walk.

Three or four days before we left Tomsk for Irkútsk, Mr. Frost and I, by invitation of Captain Gudím, the officer in charge of the Tomsk convoy command, drove to the forwarding prison at 7 A.M. to see the departure of a marching party. As we drew up before the prison we saw that the party had not yet made its appearance and we sat in our *dróshky* watching the scenes at the gate. On each side of the lead-colored portal was a long wooden bench, upon which half a dozen soldiers, in dark green uniforms, were sitting in lazy attitudes, waiting for the party to come out. An occasional high-pitched jingle of chains could be heard from within the inclosure, and now and then half of the double gate was thrown open to admit a couple of fettered convicts carrying water in a large wooden bucket slung between them on a shoulder-pole. Every person who entered the prison yard was hastily searched from head to foot by one of the two sentries at the gate, in order to prevent the smuggling in of prohibited articles, and especially of *vódka*.

About eight o'clock *telégas* for the transportation of the weak and infirm began to gather in the street in front of the prison; a shabby under-officer who had been lounging with the soldiers on one of the benches rose, yawned, and went discontentedly into the prison courtyard; the soldiers put on their blanket-rolls and picked up their rifles; and a louder and more continuous jingling of chains from the other side of the palisade announced that the convict party was assembling. At last the prison blacksmith came out, bringing a small portable forge, a lap anvil, a hammer, and an armful of chains and leg-fetters, which he threw carelessly on the ground beside him; the soldiers shouldered their guns and took positions in a semicircle so as to form a cordon; an under-officer with the muster-roll of the party in his hand and another with a leather bag of copper coins

153

slung over his shoulder stationed themselves at the gate; and at the word "Gatóva" [Ready] the convicts, in single file, began to make their appearance. The officer with the muster-roll checked off the prisoners as they answered to their names; the blacksmith, with the aid of a soldier, examined the leg-fetters to see that the rivets were fast and that the bands could not be slipped over the heel; and, finally the second under-officer gave to every man ten cents in copper coin for two days's subsistence. When all the hard-labor convicts, had come out of the prison yard, they arranged themselves in two parallel lines so that they could be conveniently counted, and removed their caps so that the under-officer could see that their heads had been half shaved as required by law. They were then dismissed and the penal colonists, went through the same routine—the soldiers of the convoy stepping backward and extending the limits of their cordon as the number of prisoners outside the palisade gradually increased.

At length the whole party, numbering 350 or 400, was assembled in the street. Every prisoner had a gray linen bag in which he stored his scanty personal effects; many of them were provided with copper kettles which dangled from their leg-fetter chains; and one convict was carrying to the mines in his arms a small brown dog.

"All prisoners who have certificates from the doctor, step out!" shouted Captain Gudím, and twenty-five or thirty "incapables"— some old and infirm, some pale and emaciated from sickness— separated themselves from the main body of convicts in the road. An under-officer collected and examined their certificates, and as fast as their cases were approved they climbed into *telégas*. One man, although apparently sick, was evidently a malingerer, since, as he took his place in a partly filled *teléga,* he was greeted with a storm of groans and hoots from the whole convict party.

The number of prisoners who, when they leave Tomsk, are unable to walk is sometimes very large. In the year 1884, 658 *telégas* were loaded there with exiles of this class, and as every *teléga* held four persons the aggregate number of "incapables" must have exceeded 2500. Such a state of things, of course, is the natural result of the overcrowding of the Tomsk forwarding prison.

When the sick and infirm had all taken the places assigned them in the invalid carts, Captain Gudím took off his cap, crossed himself and bowed in the direction of the prison church, and then, turning to the convicts, cried, "Well, boys! Go ahead! A safe journey to you!"

"Party—to the right! Party—march!" shouted one of the under-officers, and with a clinking of chains which sounded like the jingling of innumerable bunches of keys the gray throng, hemmed in by a cordon of soldiers, began its long journey of 1800 miles to the mines of the Trans-Baikál. The marching convicts, who took the lead, were closely followed by the *telégas* with the sick and the infirm; next came three or four carts loaded with gray linen bags; and, finally, in a *tárántas* [a carriage], behind the rear guard of soldiers, Captain Gudím. The column moved at the rate of about two miles an hour; and long before noon it was enveloped in a suffocating cloud of dust raised by the shuffling, fetter-incumbered feet of the prisoners.

1892

A FAMINE-STRICKEN VILLAGE
by Paul von Birukoff

DURING THE WINTER of 1891–1892, millions of Russian peasants were starving. The immediate cause of the famine was the bad harvest of the preceding year; but the disaster had its roots in the malfunctioning of the well-meaning Alexander IIs' decree of 1861 by which he liberated the serfs. Previously, even a cruel landowner had a direct interest in the health of his peasants since, in a manner of speaking, they were his "property." But, once freed, the peasant was on his own, most of the time with a plot of land that was too small to support him and his family. Added to this bad state of affairs was the high rate of taxation and the ruthless methods of the Tsar's tax collectors. A Swedish investigator reports one instance where "the 'fatherly government' seized the last provisions of the destitute peasants, in the shape of 300 hens and sold them to a rich money-lender at about a penny a piece to pay off arrears of taxes."

Leo Tolstoy tried for years to intercede for the peasants with the government. In 1892, he went himself to the famine area and, with a band of devoted followers, took an active part in organizing relief work. Paul von Birukoff, a young Russian nobleman, was one of this band. He went to the district of Samara, in the heart of the steppe country, opened soup kitchens, and helped the stricken peasants to survive the crisis.

It is a fresh spring morning. The sun is not yet risen. I go out into the streets to breathe the pure morning air. The village folk are beginning to stir. As the peasant women light the fires in their ovens slender columns of smoke ascend. The church bells are ringing for matins, and a number of old men and women are going, single file, into the church. Half-wakened, uncombed *mushik* [peasant]-youths crawl slowly from the low *izbas* [log huts] to harness the horses and fetch water. From other huts come peasant men and women with yokes on their shoulders.

The earth is hard in the morning frost. From the distance comes the ring of a horse's hoofs striking the frozen ground. It is most likely someone riding out on the steppes to relieve the horsekeeper, who has been tending the village horses on the hills where the snow has melted, and the poor beasts munch the sparse and short stubble left from last year's harvest, or the dried old grass roots. "They may find something," think the *mushiks;* so they keep one horse at home, to fetch water and for other household purposes, while they take it in turns to watch the others out on the steppes. However poor the feeding is out there it is better than at home, where everything is devoured, even to the rotten straw on the roofs of the outhouses, and in many places of the *izbas* also.

I return home, and sit down to the perusal of lists and accounts in connection with the different branches of our relief work among the starving folk. The most pressing need of the day is for seedcorn. A peasant enters, makes the usual sign of the cross and bows as he turns to the "holy corner."

"What is your need?"

"Please put down my name for sowing-corn."

"But will you not get it from the official committee?"

"I have no horse, little father. They gave me no rye in the autumn, and I could not sow. They frighten me by saying I shall get nothing. What shall I do—perish? We are eight in family. Don't forsake me, little *kormiletz"* (one who gives food), adds the peasant with quivering voice. I see him sink upon his knees. I get him up with difficulty, write down his need, and send him away.

The same moment comes another peasant with rolling gait, clumsy, rough, pale, and exhausted.

"I come to your worthiness—to ask your grace for seedcorn."

"Do you get anything from the committee?"

"Your worship, what can I get from that quarter? We are seven in family; my wife, four girls, and the boy one year old, and I hear they give two *pud* (80 pounds) for each 'male soul.' So I shall only get two *pud.* How can I keep my family on that? Everything is sold and eaten up. I have no horse nor cow. I have hired myself out to a rich peasant to plough his field, and for this I shall plough my own little plot with his oxen, but I have no seed to sow with." I write his name on the list for further consideration.

A woman comes in sobbing. "My little father—"

"What do you want?"

"My husband is very ill—his body is beginning to swell—he

157

cannot climb down from the oven. Help us, little father, for Christ's sake! I have tried everything already; I have covered him with cow-dung, given him cherry-balsam, sprinkled him with holy water."

"Where do you live?"

"Little father, I live near the small stream, in the narrow lane, the third hut. Come little good-giver."

I promise I will, and enter her name.

Then come others, each with a special request.

I go for a while to get tea with my landlady, and then go out. The noon bell is ringing. I turn my steps to the *izba* in which one of the five free eating-rooms is established. As I enter I hear the *molitva* (grace) being sung. The last word is slowly sung as I come in.

The guests salute each other, take their spoons and sit down at three tables. There are forty persons present. The servers pour the soup into large wooden bowls, and distribute equal-sized bits of bread to each guest. All sit down and in quiet orderliness begin to eat.

"Here is no famine," I said to myself. Is it such a simple thing to satisfy the wants of men, to give them a piece of bread and a bowl of warm soup? And I remember how intricate is the process by which bread and warm soup come to the mouth of a starving man. Long rows of carts, freight trains, flour merchants, etc. rush through my imagination.

I return home to dinner. Several peasants are already gathered there. I inquire into their needs, write down their names, and dismiss them. In the afternoon I go out once more, and recollect the woman with the sick husband. I make for her home, and, with great difficulty, try to find her earth-hut. At last I am clearly at the lane spoken of. The hut must be there, but beyond the fence I see only a snowdrift, darkened a little under the warmth of the spring sun. I find that the drift is really the clay hut buried in snow; in this the

158

family Koroljoff lives, eight persons. Stooping down, I creep through the low door, and enter the hut. A damp and suffocating air meet me, so that I am near fainting. A few rays of light struggle with difficulty through a small window, for which an opening has been dug in the snow.

The woman who had come to me is at the oven, busy with a stone jar in her hand. Behind her two little children, covered with rags, pale and dirty, are sitting on a bench, sucking a hard crust. In another corner something is lying on a bench, covered with a battered sheepskin cloak. A small girl, about ten years old, sits at the side, nursing a small child.

"Where is your husband?" I ask, after greeting.

"On the oven, little father."

At the same time the sick man comes scrambling from the oven, moaning as he totters with great difficulty to the bench, and by the aid of his wife sits down by the table, resting his head on both hands so that he almost lies across it.

"How have you got into such a bad plight? What do you eat? Do you get anything from the committee?"

"We get something, little father, but it is not enough. It was too little from the first. Then we borrowed. When we got more from the committee we had first to pay back what we had borrowed, so that there remained still less than before. The first week of the month we have enough to still our hunger, but the other weeks we have to starve. What have we not eaten! We dug clay, which we mixed with a little flour, but all kinds of clay are not suitable."

I listen to this story in silence. What can I say to these people, who have been reduced to such a condition that they discriminate between two kinds of clay—eatable and not eatable?

I go out into the fresh air, which I inhale in deep draughts. I feel as if my body, unaccustomed to this polluted, suffocating

159

atmosphere was poisoned; yet in this air a whole family is living and growing up! I know, too, that there are many such families; I have seen numbers of them myself.

1900s

ON LEO TOLSTOY
by Maxim Gorky

THIS DESCRIPTION of "life with Tolstoy" when he was an old and famous man was written by Maxim Gorky, himself a writer of distinction. It is interesting not only as a portrait of Tolstoy but also as a study of Gorky.

The two men could not have been more different as regards background and character. In contrast to Tolstoy, Gorky was a man of the people. Where Gorky had talent, Tolstoy had genius, and where Gorky was a practical revolutionist, Tolstoy was a mystic and a dreamer. This difference in character and point of view led to a somewhat ambiguous friendship in which admiration alternated with irritation and the sympathetic understanding of the fellow artist, with the impatience of the proletarian for the aristocrat.

One hot day he overtook me on the low road. He was riding in the direction of Livadia, mounted on a quiet little Tartar horse. Grey and shaggy, in a light, white, mushroom-shaped felt hat, he looked very much like a gnome.

Holding back his horse he hailed me, and I walked along by his side, telling him, among other things, that I had just had a letter from V. G. Korolenko. Tolstoy shook his beard angrily.

"Does he believe in God?" he asked.

"I do not know."

"That means you do not know the chief thing about him. He is a believer, but he is afraid to admit it in front of atheists."

When we came to the edge of the estate belonging to the Grand Duke A. M. Romanoff, we met three Romanoffs who were standing talking on the road, very close to each other. The road was blocked by a one-horse vehicle, and a saddled horse was standing a little to one side. Leo Nicolaevich [Tolstoy] could not pass between them. He stared sternly and expectantly at the Romanoffs, but they had turned aside when he came up. At length the saddled horse pranced nervously and stepped aside, allowing Tolstoy's horse to pass.

After riding on in silence for some minutes he exclaimed: "They recognised me, the fools." And added, a few moments later: "That horse knew that it must make way for Tolstoy!"

In spite of the monotony of his preaching, what infinite variety is to be found in this almost legendary man! In the park, to-day, when he was talking with Mullah of Haspre, he behaved like a trusting, simple-minded, little peasant, for whom the time has arrived when he must take thought for his last days. Small of stature and shrivelled up, he appeared beside the broad, corpulent Tartar, like a little old man whose soul has just awakened to the sense of something that lay buried within it, and who feared the questions which that awakening might bring.

He lifted his shaggy eyebrows in amazement, blinking slyly with his piercing little eyes, and extinguishing the intolerably penetrating fire which burnt within them. His all-seeing eye was rivetted upon the broad face of the Mullah, the pupil losing the sharpness which so confused people.

To the Mullah he put childish questions on the meaning of life, on the soul and on God, substituting the verses of the Bible and the Prophets for the verses of the Koran with incredible agility. Al-

161

together he was acting with the marvellous skill of which only a man who is at once a great artist and a great sage is capable.

Again, a few days ago, when he was talking about music to Tanijeff and Suler, he went into raptures over it like a child. One could see that he was admiring his own enthusiasm, or, to be more precise, his capacity for enthusiasm. He held that Schopenhauer had written more wisely and profoundly about music than anyone else; and described music as "the dumb prayer of the soul."

"Why dumb?" asked Suler.

"Because it uses no words. There is more soul in a sound than there is in a thought. A thought is like a purse—it contains pennies, mere trifles, while a sound remains unsoiled—pure through and through."

With evident delight and in charming, simple words, he expressed his ideas, choosing—this was unusual with him—the finest and most tender he could think of. And unexpectedly smiling into his beard, he murmured softly, caressingly:

"All musicians are stupid people, and the more gifted the musician, the more shallow he is. It is curious that they should all be so pious."

When you speak to Tolstoy of things which he can put to no use, he listens with indifference and incredulity. In fact he does not ask—he merely inquires. Like a collector of valuable curios, he only collects things which are in keeping with the rest of the collection.

One day he was sorting his letters:

"They all make a great fuss about me," he said, "writing and so on. But in the end, when I die, in a year or so, people will say: 'Tolstoy? Ah, that is the count who tried to make boots; and then something curious happened to him. Is that the fellow you mean?' "

One never tires of speculating about him, but it is trying to meet him often. Personally I should find it impossible to live in the same house with him, not to mention in the same room. His surroundings become like a desert where everything is scorched by the sun and the sun itself is smouldering away, threatening a black and eternal night.

1904

SIBERIA
by Jules Legras

THE CONQUEST of Siberia did not really get under way until late in the sixteenth century. It was led by the Cossacks who founded towns and established military colonies without being too squeamish as regards the treatment they meted out to any of the stray groups of Siberian inhabitants that happened to cross their way. By the end of the seventeenth century, Russia had already hit upon the policy of colonizing the vast, cold country to the east by what might be called the "exile system." Russians of all classes were sentenced to exile in Siberia for every sort of minor offense. Later on, whole generations of socialists contributed a large quota of intellectuals to the pool of immigrants. Between 1823 and 1898 no fewer than 700,000 exiles accompanied by 216,000 voluntary followers trekked eastward; and, after the revolution of 1905, 45,000 political exiles alone arrived to settle the still sparsely populated country.

Jules Legras was one of the group of brilliant young Frenchmen who accompanied Theophile Gautier on his trip to Russia in 1904.

A few years ago Cheliabinsk was only a little village, but the building of the railroad has invested it with an ever-increasing importance. At one time not even a postal station, and outside of the great road of travel, it has become all at once the advance post of a colossal iron ribbon. Everything that enters Siberia and everything that leaves it by land must stop here.

Cheliabinsk, too, is the first stopping point of the Russian emigrants who come each year in such great numbers to colonise Asia. Indeed emigration was the strongest argument put forth by Russia for the construction of the railroad, and there is an annual exodus from Russia of no less than two or three hundred thousand peasants.

The place of departure occupies a great enclosure in which snow-covered log buildings are scattered among the white birch-trees. There are dormitories, refectories, infirmaries, kitchens and bath-houses. And although at this season the emigration, properly speaking, has not yet begun, and numbers but the belated ones of the last summer or those who are returning displeased with their venture, the place is full. Fancy an oblong hall around which runs a sort of sloping table about seven feet in width. This table serves both as seat and bed to the occupants of the place. The furniture is similar to that used in prisons and lodging-houses, but it is difficult to move about owing to the baggage scattered pell mell on the floor alongside the proprietors. Outside the cold is very great, in spite of the brilliant sunshine. As one opens the door, a cloud of vapor greets one, as if from a steam-bath; the heat is suffocating, and the air extremely difficult to breathe. On the "table" half-nude figures are stretched in shocking confusion. The children wear but a little shirt falling to their knees; the men are dressed in trousers and shirt, over which, should they desire to go out, they put a heavy sheepskin cloak; the women have on a cotton chemise and a skirt. The Russian peasants adore a stifling atmosphere, like that which reigns here; when they go out, they dress warmly but indoors they often are nearly naked. Our entrance was the signal for perfect silence, interrupted only by snores, coughing and children's cries. The men rose, and the children gazed with curiosity at us; but the women, in absolute indifference, continued uninterruptedly their occupations.

On the table, on which with the coming of night everyone stretches out, lay indescribable bundles of rags, while from all this heaped-up humanity and misery there exhaled a nauseating odor that turned one giddy.

I should like to repeat a conversation that I had one evening last year with several "politicals" on the subject of their exile. Yielding to my entreaties that day, all determined to answer my questions. D—, the first to speak, had been transported one fine day with a friend, without knowing the reason, into a little hamlet in the heart of the forests of Northern Russia, but neither he nor his companions in exile could receive permission to give lessons. The exercise of teaching is rigorously forbidden to those who are called the "politicals." Finally his friend became a shoe-maker; while he himself, having at one time in leisure moments amused himself by learning the trade of locksmith, joined two locksmiths from St. Petersburg, themselves also exiled in this hole of a place, and together they opened a shop, where at first they undertook to repair, but finally to make guns, locks, samovars, even watches.

Another of my friends, a great brown man, A—, had been sent to a Siberian village in the basin of the Yenesei. Two others accompanied him, who were wheelwrights; he himself was a student of medicine. The three all together had twenty dollars in money and ten in debts. Arrived towards the end of September, they employed the month of October in building an isba. Once in the house they set to work. Most of the income was furnished by A—. A student of medicine in his third year, he did his best to help the sick who flocked to him, for, in the opinion of the poor creatures of these forsaken countries, every civilized man is a doctor. He would not accept money for his visits, but left his patients to give what they thought best. Although these peasants were very poor, their gifts sufficed to more than support the three friends. But this prosperity was not of long duration. A— was forced to abandon the use of his profession, for lack of ability to overcome the ignorance of his clients. The peasants wanted to strike bargains, to pay so much to be cured at such a time and in such a fashion! In the end A— went to work with a cabinetmaker. To-day he is free.

A third speaker, whose brilliant eyes shone behind his glasses, took the story in his turn. It was the good T—. "The history of my adventures in Siberia are less gay," said he, "than those you have just heard. Our friends have not spoken of the horrors of their isolation, nor the tortures of the journey. I was very young when I was sent here, and had many illusions, and they helped me to endure everything. Perhaps one of the incidents of our slow journey may interest you. With us, as we walked to-wards the boundaries of Asia, was an old Jew, an excellent man who spoke neither Russian, Polish, nor German, but only a Hebrew patois. He was as peaceable as he was indifferent to any form of government, still he walked with us, 'the politicals.' And this is the reason. In a little town in South-western Russia, this man kept a sort of little inn, which was frequented from motives of economy by very poor people. One day a search was made of his house, and amongst others, a letter was found addressed under his name to one of his customers. The letter was compromising. Our man was arrested without chance of explanation, and sent off. As for myself, I had about six dollars a month to live upon in a little out-of-the-way village, where barley was worth twenty francs. I had to learn how to make bread. One of my friends and I studied it from a little school book, for we were profoundly ignorant of the rudiments of the bakery. We made use of a sort of rye flour. The peasants around us baked their bread each day; in order to have time for our studies, we attempted to bake but twice a week, but the bread when stale was so indigestible and the flour so coarse it gave us dysentery. We lived down there in the most absolute isolation, in the midst of whites more ignorant than savages. But gradually they became accustomed to us. We used to read them Turgenieff's 'Stories Of A Hunter,' and when the book was finished we had to begin again. It was a great success," concluded T— with a smile full of sadness.

I am far from desiring to give sensational stories, but these will serve to explain the formation of the most cultivated and honorable portion of Siberian society. A quarter of a century has passed away since they first began to suffer, and now they are men with families, and a position among the most respected citizens of the towns in which they reside. They worked hard in a hard country; now they scatter around them the good seed of instruction, together with the noblest examples of civic virtues in a corrupt society, which is gradually being modified under their influence. These stories are not mere anecdotes; they are typical facts.

1904

THE WAR BETWEEN RUSSIA AND JAPAN
by Count Leo Tolstoy

FOR SOME YEARS Russia and Japan had been rivals for power in the Far East. Russia had gained possession of Sakhalin Island, had built the Trans-Siberian Railroad joining St. Petersburg and Vladivostok, and, in the wake of the Boxer Rebellion in China, had obtained practical control of Manchuria. Japan had watched all these Russian maneuvers with increasing uneasiness; but when Russia began to covet the use of the Korean harbors, which were almost within gunshot of the Japanese coast, the long-brewing distrust erupted into a crisis.

After five months of unsuccessful negotiation, the Japanese fleet struck at the Russian Pacific squadron with no advance warning. War was declared in February 1904; by September 1905 Russia had been decisively defeated.

From the outset the war was unpopular in Russia. Leo Tolstoy, pacifist and visionary Christian, whose faith in universal love was incompatible with war of any kind, was one of the first men to raise his voice in eloquent protest. His essay, "The War Between Russia and Japan," is especially interesting for the insight it gives us into the thought and feelings of the "common man," the peasant-turned-soldier.

Again war. Again sufferings, necessary to nobody, utterly uncalled for; again fraud, again the universal stupefaction and brutalisation of men.

Yesterday I met a Reservist soldier, accompanied by his mother and wife. All three were riding in a cart; he had had a drop too much; his wife's face was swollen with tears. He turned to me:

"Goodbye to thee! Lyof Nicholaevitch; off to the Far East."

"Well, art thou going to fight?"

"Well, someone has to fight!"

"No one need fight!"

He reflected for a moment. "But what is one to do, where can one escape?"

"Where can one escape?" That is the precise expression of that mental condition which, in the official and journalistic world, is translated into the words—"For the Faith, the Tsar, and the Fatherland." Those who, abandoning their hungry families, go to suffering, to death, say as they feel: "Where can one escape?" Whereas those who sit in safety in their luxurious palaces say that all Russian men are ready to sacrifice their lives for their adored monarch and for the glory and greatness of Russia.

Yesterday, from a peasant I know, I received two letters, one after the other.

This is the first:

"Dear Lyof Nicholaevitch: Well, to-day I have received the official announcement of my call to the service; to-morrow I must present myself at the headquarters. That is all. And after that—to the Far East to meet the Japanese bullets.

"About my own, and my household's, grief I will not tell you. It is not you who will fail to understand all the horror of my position and the horrors of war; all this you have long ago painfully realised, and you understand it all. What is my wife to do now with her four children? As an old man, of course, you cannot do anything yourself for my folks, but you might ask some of your friends in their leisure to visit my orphaned family. I beg you earnestly that if my wife proves unable to bear the agony of her helplessness with her burden of children, and makes up her mind to go to you for help and counsel, you will receive and console her.

"I was not able to resist the summons, but I say beforehand that through me not one Japanese family shall be orphaned. My God! how dreadful is all this—how painful to abandon all by which one lives and in which one is concerned."

The second letter is as follows:

"Kindest Lyof Nicholaevitch:

"Only one day of actual service has passed, and I have already lived through an eternity of most desperate torments. From 8 o'clock in the morning till 9 in the evening we have been crowded and knocked about to and fro in the barrack yard like a herd of cattle, the comedy of medical examination was three times repeated, and those who had reported themselves ill did not receive even ten minutes' attention before they were marked 'Satisfactory.' When we, these two thousand satisfactory individuals, were driven from the military commander to the barracks, along the road spread out for almost a verst stood a crowd of relatives, mothers, and wives with infants in arms, and if you had only heard and seen how they clasped their fathers, husbands, sons, and, hanging round their necks, wailed hopelessly! Generally I behave in a restrained way, and can restrain my feelings, but I could not hold out, and I also wept." (In journalistic language this same is expressed thus: "The upheaval of patriotic feeling is immense.")

"Where can one escape!"

Meanwhile those who remain at home not only feel this, but know and express it. Yesterday in the high road I met some peasants returning from Toula. One of them was reading a leaflet as he walked by the side of his cart.

I asked: "What is that?—a telegram?"

"This is yesterday's, but here is one of to-day."

We stopped. I read it.

"What do we want with this Manchuria, or whatever it is called? There is sufficient land here. And what a lot of people and of property has been destroyed."

Yes, the relation of men to war is now quite different from that which formerly existed even so lately as the year '77.

The papers set forth that, during the receptions of the Tsar, who is travelling about Russia for the purpose of hypnotising the men who are being sent to murder, indescribable enthusiasm is manifested among the people. As a matter of fact something quite different is being manifested. From all sides one hears reports that in one place three Reservists have hanged themselves; in another spot two more. The words "For the Faith, the King, and the Fatherland," the National Anthem and shouts of "Hurrah!" no longer act upon people as they once did.

Yesterday the news came in of the sinking of the Japanese ironclads, and in the so-called higher circles of Russian fashionable, rich, intellectual society, they are, without the slightest conscientious scruples, rejoicing at the destruction of a thousand human lives. Yet, to-day I have received from a simple seaman, a man standing on the lowest plane of society, the following letter:

"Much respected Lyof Nicholaevitch, I greet you with a low bow, with love, much respected Lyof Nicholaevitch.

I have been a great lover of reading your works. Well, Lyof Nicholaevitch, we are now in a state of war; please write to me whether it is agreeable to God or not, that our commanders compel us to kill. I pray you, Lyof Nicholaevitch, have you got any books from which I could see whether truth exists on earth or not? Send me such books. What they cost, I will pay. Goodbye for the present. I remain alive and well, and wish the same to you from the Lord God."

There follows the address—Port Arthur, the name of the ship on which the correspondent serves, his rank, and his name.

In a direct way, in words, I cannot answer this dear, serious, and truly enlightened man. He is in Port Arthur, with which there is no longer any communication either by letter or telegraph. But we still have a mutual means of communication. This means is that God, in whom we both believe, and concerning whom we both know, that war is not according to His will. The doubt which has arisen in his soul contains at the same time its own solution. And this doubt has now arisen and is living in the souls of thousands and thousands of men, not only Russians, and not only Japanese, but all those unfortunate people who are compelled by violence to fulfil the act most repellent to human nature.

The doubt as to "whether or not it be agreeable to God that our compatriots compel us to kill"—this is a spark of that fire which Jesus kindled upon earth and which is beginning to spread. To know and feel this is a great joy.

Leo Tolstoy,

Yasnaya Polyana, May 21, 1904.

1905

THE MOSCOW RISING
by Henry W. Nevinson

THE YEAR 1905 marked a new phase in the history of the long revolutionary struggle that had slowly been gathering force inside
Russia. Until the Moscow Rising, the intelligentsia, students,
journalists and other professional men, had worked alone in secret
societies and in the underground; had endured imprisonment and
exile in their struggle to bring freedom to an autocratic country and
help the downtrodden workers and peasants achieve at least a
minimum of comfort and security. But in the last week of December
1905, when a shooting revolution spread through Moscow, the intelligentsia were joined at the barricades by the workers. The street
fighting went on for days and was only put down at last by guard
battalions hastily marched into the city from outside. For the time
being they succeeded in quelling the revolutionists; but the Moscow
Rising was a prophetic dress rehearsal of a more successful revolution that was to come only twelve years later.

Henry Nevinson, from whose book the following account of the
Moscow Rising was taken, spent the year 1905–1906 in Russia as
special correspondent for a British newspaper.

I went for half a mile along the continuation of the Dmitrovka, and
from end to end I found it crowded with work-people of the better
class, all intensely excited and alert, and apparently all enthusiastic
for the movement. The whole long street had been admirably barri-
caded, and as it runs towards the Petrovsky Park and the open country, it seemed likely that it had been specially prepared as a line of
retreat in case of disaster. Barricades were erected every thirty yards,
and in one place the whole of the electric train had been drawn at
right angles across the road in three lines, making far the largest
barricade then existing in the world. Four red flags flew from its

summit, and upon the largest flag some girl had stitched the white letters "For Freedom."

I made a short cut for home by way of the Flower Boulevard. But as I was going along its valley towards the Ermitage, four big flashes in front, looking very orange in the twilight, warned me that guns had been brought down there to demolish the series of barricades running across the gardens where I was. Men and girls were throwing them up with devoted zeal, sawing through telegraph poles, wrenching ironwork from its sockets, and dragging out the planks from builders' yards.

In expectation of sudden death, all the students, both men and girls, had stitched little labels inside the back of their coats, so that when they were killed, their parents might possibly hear the news. I think most of the revolutionists had done the same, but the dead were piled up and carted into the country for burial with such indiscriminate carelessness, that I doubt if the precaution was of very much avail.

In many battles there comes a moment when little or nothing appears to have changed, and yet you suddenly realize that all is over but the running. Such a moment came on the morning of Christmas Day as I went up the Sadovaya towards the central revolutionist position where I had been the afternoon before. The barricades were still standing, the Sadovaya was still covered with such a network of wire about four feet from the ground that one had to walk under it bent double like a hoop, and no horse could have moved. The guns had not come perceptibly nearer, and in the centre of the town I had seen an officer stopped and deprived of his sword by half a dozen men with revolvers, who threatened to strip him naked, as another had been stripped the day before. There were rumours of all manner of wild enterprises on foot—attacks on stations, on prisons, on barracks. All these were favorable signs. Yet as I went along, I suddenly realised "instinctively" as it is called, that the tide had turned, and that the highest moment of revolutionary success lay behind us.

The guns began firing heavily again about eleven. I turned down the main Boulevard westward. The further I went, the more disturbed and dangerous the atmosphere of things became. Something evidently was happening down that way. Troops were marching hastily about and two guns passed at full gallop. At one place I heard an officer's voice shouting some order, and the few people on the pavement near me began to run for their lives.

New barricades were rapidly appearing across many of the streets leading down into the Boulevard from the right hand, or north-west side. It was only after two or three days that I understood the real significance of this movement, by which the revolutionists were preparing for their final stand in the extreme north-west of the city.

Yet the crisis, as I had felt in the morning, was really over. When I passed through the middle of the city, and on to my own quarter, the crowds were still running to and fro in panic around the Theatre Square, men and women were still falling unexpectedly in the streets, there was as much to do as ever helping the wounded, and the ambulance yards were continually being filled. But the life seemed to have dropped out of the rising. People were talking with terror of a great peasant invasion, hundreds and thousands strong, that was already marching to deliver the Little Mother Moscow. With better reason they said that Mischenko, the hero of the Japanese war, was coming as military governor with 7,000 Cossacks. Hour by hour the citizens were agitated by new alarms, and the cautious began to think enough had been done for freedom. That night the revolutionists issued appeals calling for volunteers at six shillings a day and a revolver.

During the next two days there was very little outward change in the position except that the feeling of disaster grew. The guns still sprinkled bullets over the barricades and wrecked the houses on each side. The soldiers continued their slow and perilous advance from street to street. People fell at random; the hospital and ambulances were crowded beyong limits. On the Tuesday evening an official estimate put the killed and wounded between 8,000 and 9,000. For the first time I heard revolutionists beginning to describe the whole movement as a dress rehearsal and to congratulate themselves upon the excellent practise in street fighting which they had enjoyed.

An hour or two before daylight next day, I had to go to a house on the further side of the Sadovaya to help bring provisions to an English family. Some of the barricades were on fire or gently smouldering; the rest stood deserted. The pavements were strewn with glass and bricks. Houses on both sides were ruined with shell. Some were burning.

For the rest of that day the guns and soldiers were engaged in clearing the quarter of barricades, entanglements and all. It was an easy task now, though the firing was more violent than ever, as the progress was more rapid. For the revolutionists had received orders from their committee that morning to abandon the street fighting and scatter to their homes or out into the country, continuing the propaganda and holding themselves ready for the next opportunity. Some escaped, at least for the time. Some refused to obey, but continued the fighting. Many were seized, and for days afterwards small parties of soldiers or police in every street drove some unhappy creature in front of them with his hands tied. What became of these prisoners, we only suspected at the time; we found out later. On this part of the Moscow rising, there is no more to chronicle but massacre. And so the barricades and their defenders faded into history, and law and order were restored.

THE FIRST DUMA
by Maurice Baring

IN THE WAKE of the disastrous war with Japan and the widespread unrest that for the first time was powerful enough to threaten the untrammeled power of the Tsar, the embattled ruler issued a Manifesto (October 30th, 1905) which granted certain primary liberties to the Russian people and established a representative assembly, the Duma. On May 10th, 1906, this first representative body, elected by the Russian people, met in St. Petersburg at the Tauris Palace which had once belonged to Potemkin, Catherine the Great's minister and lover.

The first act of the Duma was to write an address to the Throne in which it advocated proposals for the reform of practically every field of public life. Alarmed by what seemed to him a too radical approach to Russia's problems, the Tsar appointed a new premier, a provincial governor called Stolypin. He was a man of forceful character, entirely loyal to the Russian monarchy. By a series of devious maneuvers, Stolypin managed to get the original Duma dissolved and to have a more conservative one elected to replace it. But nothing could take away from the May 10th Duma the honor of being the first Russian Assembly to have been elected by popular vote.

I had the good fortune to gain admission to the Duma yesterday afternoon. I think it is the most interesting sight I have ever seen. When you arrive at the Tauris Palace, which outside has an appearance of dignified stateliness, the stateliness of the Eighteenth Century, you walk through a spacious front hall into what looks like a gigantic white ball-room built in the late Louis XVI. style. This is the lobby; beyond it is the Hall of the Duma itself. In this long gallery members and visitors were already flocking, walking up and down, talking, and smoking cigarettes and throwing the ashes and the ends on the polished floor. One saw peasants in their long black coats, some of them wearing military medals and crosses; popes [priests], Tartars, Poles, men in every kind of dress except uniforms. When the sitting began I went up into the gallery. The Hall of the Duma itself is likewise white, delicate in decoration, an essentially gentlemanlike room. The sitting began about three o'clock. The members go to their appointed places, on which their cards are fixed, and the impression of diversity of dress and type becomes still stronger and more picturesque.

You see dignified old men in frock coats, aggressively democratic-looking "intelligents," with long hair and pince-nez, a Polish bishop dressed in purple, who looks like the Pope; men without collars; members of the proletariate, men in loose Russian shirts with belts; and men dressed in the costume of two centuries ago. The President walked in to his seat under the portrait of the Emperor [Nicholas II], which is a rather shiny study in blue and white.

The President, C. A. Muromzev, strikes one as dignity itself. He exercises his functions with perfect serenity and absolute fairness. After reading congratulatory telegrams from various parts of the Empire he proceeded to read a motion proposed by a workman of the Government of Moscow that before proceeding further a telegram should be sent to the Emperor asking for a general amnesty for political offenders, and another motion asking for an immediate amnesty, proposed by a peasant. A debate ensued. The speeches were sensible and moderate. What struck me most in the speeches I heard was the naturalness of their tone, and the absence of declamatory rhetoric. A second thing which struck me was the respect and the instantaneous obedience shown to the President; when he called to order by ringing his bell the silence was immediate and complete. Soon after four o'clock the Duma proceeded to elect the thirty-three members by whom the Reply to the Address is to be drawn up. The members poured into the gallery and everywhere small groups collected discussing various matters.

177

Many of the small groups where the discussion was being carried on were interesting. One heard violent ideas and wild words being bandied about. One peasant said to a friend of mine: "When I look upon this palace my blood boils; it was built out of the blood and sweat of the poor." So it was. "Then you are a person who nurses hatred?" said my friend. "Yes," he answered, "I hate, hate, hate the rich!" Another man told a lady of my acquaintance that he was a Socialist. She asked him if he was in favour of the land being made over to the State. He said "No." He explained his views which were really rather those of an extreme Radical than a Socialist. "But you are not a Socialist?" "Yes, I am," he answered; and asked her who she was. She said that she was the daughter of a Count who is a member of the Duma. "I am pleased to have spoken with a Countess," he answered, perfectly simply.

My impression of the whole is that the Duma is far more moderate than I expected. And I think that the future violence or moderation of the Duma will depend very largely on the action of the higher authorities, and of what is at present the official Government.

Yesterday a peasant said in his speech: "We hear it said that we have millions of men behind us, and we must demand, not ask; these high-sounding phrases are very well for a private meeting, but are out of place in the Duma." This was a very sensible thing to say; but it is true, nevertheless, that the Duma has the whole country behind it. Another peasant, speaking at a small meeting a few days ago, said: "Russia has waited for the Duma as the chosen people had waited for the Messiah. Will they dare to crucify it? No, they will not dare. For who would be the Pilate? The Emperor will not be the Pilate, for, if he were to call for water in which to wash his hands, he would have to wash his hands, not in the waters of the Neva, but in the blood of the whole Russian people."

178

1906

ODESSA
by Harry de Windt

In 1906, Harry de Windt, an experienced journalist, was sent to
Russia as special correspondent for the *Westminster Gazette*. Traveling through the Balkan States as well as through Russia, Mr. de
Windt summed up his impressions of the journey in the title of
his book, *Through Savage Europe*. After reading his account of his
experiences with the police at Odessa, as well as his encounter with
the superstitions of the peasantry, one cannot help but sympathize
with the uncomplimentary title.

Odessa is certainly the pleasantest, if not the most interesting, city in
Russia. On the arrival of the train a line regiment was drawn up
outside the station, having been hastily called out to a disturbance in
the neighbouring town; and if I have ever seen misery personified it
was in that line of grey sodden figures, devoid of all trace of martial
bearing, standing motionless in the rain, with pallid faces and down-
cast eyes. Near them a glittering group of officers, chatting and smoking cigarettes, looked gay and unconcerned; but champagne and
vodka had not cheered the departure of their men, who looked less
like soldiers than a gang of convicts bound for a city gaol!

While in Odessa I was subject to an incessant police espionage
which fully equalled my experiences on the frontier. I have put up,
as a rule, with this annoyance with equanimity (every traveller in
Russia must do so) but here it was impossible to leave the hotel for
an hour without being shadowed by an agent of the police.

The manager of the Hotel Bristol repeatedly warned his guests
to avoid Government offices and public buildings, and it was not
oversafe to walk anywhere in the streets, an official and two police-

men having been shot down on the principal boulevard within a fortnight of my arrival, during the busiest hours of the day. Indeed, it was extraordinary how little excitement was caused by tragic events of this kind—probably because of their frequency. I myself witnessed the assassination of a late chief of police, which occurrence indirectly released me from a *mauvais quart d'heure* in a police court, for at the time I had just been requested by a constable to accompany him to headquarters for carrying a "Kodak" without special permission. The afternoon was bright and sunny, and the "Daribasovka," a fashionable thoroughfare, was crowded with people. Suddenly the report of a pistol, closely followed by another, caused a number of people to rush to the spot where an elderly man in the official uniform of grey and scarlet had fallen to the ground. My policeman, now heedless of cameras, also made off like a flash of lightning to render assistance, and I discreetly and rapidly followed his example—in the opposite direction. I heard later that the wounded man eventually recovered, and the would-be assassin escaped—a sequel of such frequent occurrence that there may have been some truth in A's—assertion that many of the police were actually in league with the extreme revolutionist party.

This [Znamenka] is the center of one of the richest agricultural districts in the South, and the platform was crowded with peasants returning to their homes from a market held that day. Furs and sheepskins had been discarded in the warm spring weather, and the men wore the red shirt and velvet caftan, the women the gaily embroidered bodice and skirts of Bessarabia, where the national costume is perhaps the prettiest in Russia. Some were dancing to the merry strains of a concertina at the end of a platform, others had gathered around a little girl of about fourteen years old, who wore a silver medal with white and red ribbon which she had received for tending the sick at Port Arthur. And every one, from station officials to ragged beggars in the roadway, appeared to be nibbling pea-nuts, until closer scrutiny disclosed that they were the seeds of the sunflower, one of the most profitable harvests in Russia. Thousands of acres of these are cultivated, and the seeds are sold at an enormous profit in the shops and the streets. I found them as tasteless as bits of wood, and quite as indigestible—but so inordinate is the craving for them, especially amongst the peasantry, that most of the latter had tiny niches in their front teeth, worn away by the continual friction with the hard and gritty substance. But whether the fact was due to the sunshine or the sunflowers, everybody was happy and contented.

The superstition which prevails here amongst the peasantry is unequalled even in the remotest parts of Siberia. I recollect once entering a *traktir* on the outskirts of Rostov and remarking to the proprietor (while idly watching the gyrations of a flock of pigeons), that no man could partake daily of one of these birds for three consecutive weeks—a physical impossibility which has been proved in England by numerous attempts and inevitable failures. "Of course not," was the reply, "they are sacred birds." Throughout Russia the pigeon is regarded as sacred on account of its similarity to the symbol of the Third Person of the Trinity. And S— told me of other local superstitions, which he had observed during his journeys on business in the interior and which savour of the dark ages. Perhaps the most curious is the universal belief in the existence of a "Damovoi," a gnome-like vision which is supposed to inhabit every dwelling and render it agreeable or otherwise for the inmates. The "Damovoi's" costume is black or yellow, but he has invariably a long, grey beard, flaxen hair, and red, gleaming eyes. The remains of supper are always left on the table for the "Damovoi's" refreshment during the night, and his comfort and well-being enter into all the domestic arrangements, for if ignored in any way he takes a speedy revenge by bringing some disaster on the household. Again, over the door of every building, house or stable, there is nearly always a cross rudely scrawled in red or white paint—for no witch or evil spirit can possibly enter under that sacred emblem. In parts of Bessarabia also it is considered very unlucky to meet a "pope" or priest upon the road; but a sure way to avoid misfortune is to wait until the holy man has passed and then to walk for some distance to the right or left, crossways, behind him. But I could fill a chapter with the quaint and numerous customs practised in this part of Russia.

1911

THE AGE OF WOOD
by Stephen Graham

STEPHEN GRAHAM was a British writer who fell in love with Russia. Taking the advice of a Russian friend who told him to go north, "for there all that Russia ever was is conserved in the forests as in ice," he resolved to go to the province of Archangel. Here he lived for a whole summer, sharing the life of a primitive people and observing their customs with a sympathetic eye.

I had now left the region of the Tundra, but was still in the land of marsh and stream, where the man who loses himself in the forest comes upon strange silent lakes unknown of man and unused by him. An impressionable man, walking all day along an endless rutty forest ride, where the trees almost touch above his head, is constantly filled with terror, expectation, foreboding. But the peasant who lives there has lived this life of terror, expectation, mystery for generations. He himself is a forest mystery, a thrall and vassal of the pines.

Consider what the forest is to the moujik [peasant]. Iron, you must know, and iron-moulded and manufactured commodities are almost unknown in Archangel Province. The moujik's cradle is a pine bole, scooped out like an ancient boat. It hangs with hempen ropes from a springy sapling in his mother's cottage. His coffin is but a larger cradle, a larger, longer pine scooped out, with an axe-hewn plank to cover it, and wooden pegs to nail it down. And between the cradle and the coffin, he lives surrounded by wood. A robust baby, he clambers out of his cradle on to the pine floor, also of grand axe-hewn planks too solid to wear into holes like other poor men's floors. He crawls about till he learns to run from one solid hand-carved chair to another, and at last takes his seat at the table his father made a month before the wedding. He crosses himself to the sacred symbols painted on birch bark. He eats all his meals with a wooden spoon— forks and knifes are almost unknown in the forest. He eats off wooden plates, or out of wooden Russian basins. Even the salt-cellar is from the forest, and was plaited by his sister from reeds last year. He gets big enough to go out to the forest with his brothers and sisters, and they take birch-bark baskets and gather mushrooms or yagodi—all forest fruits are called yagodi, berries. Vania they call him, little Vania, Vashka when he looks a dirty little urchin. See him every day, in muddy little bare legs, hunting in the forest for berries, or chasing the cows who have gone astray there. He learns to walk nimbly on the uneven, moss-covered ground, and can even run among the broken branches and thorns, and leap from one dead tree to another, or swarm up the straight grey-green trunks. He learns to trap rabbits and catch young woodcocks, knows the wolf's paw, the fox paw, the bear paw in the soft soil. The priest teaches him a little in the school about God and the Tsar, and the observances of the Church, and such education suffices for Vania. He is becoming a woodsman. The forest is the best school—but he never remembers how it was he learnt there. He came to know that when the sun set it was evening, and when it rose it was morning. He learned that the foliage of a tree takes shape according to the sunshine it gets and the time of day the sunshine reaches it, and when he is in the dark forest he knows by the shape of a trunk the way out. Every tree is a compass in itself.

The time comes for Vania to marry, and he had better build himself an izba. It is of pine and three friends help him to build it, while his father stands by and directs. They have no planes and chisels, saws, squares, joiners' tables and the like. All is wrought by the axe and every joint is axe cut, and every smooth surface axe-hewn. The walls of the house and of the great stove are panelled. Vania hews out a sleeping shelf for himself and his wife above the oven. He makes unbreakable chairs to sit on and make merry, and a table, and finally, without other tool than his axe, builds a cart to take himself and his bride from the church, and he builds the shafts and the Russian collar arch to which the horse is yoked, all of wood—even the wheels are not faced with iron, and the harness is of wood and leather.

He is married at a forest church, itself forest made, built years ago by his grandfather and other villagers of their day. It is natural-shapen, a reflection in itself of the forest fir. It is not harmonious, not symmetrical—no, but then it is eye-measured; no rulers and lines were used in its construction, and not a plane or saw in cutting the planks.

Vania is wed, and at his father's house are casks of sweet beer and tubs of soaking mushrooms, and great carved bins of meal, and wooden platters full of cakes, and loving cups, and beer tankards—all of wood. Then what rejoicing, what drinking!

The time comes to scoop another cradle out of pine, and find a springy sapling to hang it from, a young fir or young birch, and it is fastened from the roof.

Human life goes on a stage, and a little baby Vania peeps into the light of day. Little Vania is put in the new cradle, and it is indeed "Hush a bye baby, on the tree top."

One night, great grandfather Vania, that is, the father of Vania's father, comes into the new house and prays to God. Then he tells them that his time is passing. He is an old man. To-morrow he will take a new log and build a coffin for himself, and he will cut a wooden cross to put above his grave. Grandfather Vania makes his coffin and puts it away till it may be necessary. Meanwhile it can hold rye-meal, or if there is little space in the old home, he can make a bed in it and sleep in it. The time will come when he will rest there all night and not awaken the next morning. Old grandfather Vania will be dead. Vania's father and Vania and other villagers will carry the coffin to the grave, and the old man's body will be committed to the ancient pine mould.

Then Vania's father, himself a grandfather, follows in the steps of Man down to the grave, and Vania ripens to his prime, and little Vania grows up and marries. All among the standing trees. Little Vania has a child, and the wheel of human life turns round a quarter-circle. So on, *da capo*.

The trees in the forest are born, grow up, are glorious, are old, are decrepit, fall down and die and sink into the moss and become earth, or perhaps become trees again, springing up in young baby trees. And the forest man likewise grows up, is glorious, becomes old, then decrepit, and he falls and dies and descends into the mossy soil. Much of his body returns to glorify God once more in tree and man.

So much, and more, is the forest to the moujik.

1900s

LENIN ON THE PLATFORM
by Leon Trotsky

Leon A. Trotsky, whose real name was Lev Davidovich Bronstein, was one of the leaders of the Bolshevik Revolution of 1917. Long a revolutionary, he had shared the hazards of that life with his fellows, undergoing the usual routine of arrest, escape and exile. He met Lenin in Europe while they were both in exile and formed a strong working partnership with him. From the time of the Revolution of 1917 until Lenin's death in 1924, Trotsky was the second most powerful man in the Soviet Union. Subsequently he was defeated by Stalin in a battle for power and was expelled from the Communist Party in 1927. From that time on he lived in exile, first in a distant part of Russia, then in Turkey and finally in Mexico, where he was murdered by a man who most people believe was an agent of the Soviet political police.

When I try mentally with fresh eye and fresh ear to see and hear Lenin on the platform, as I did the first time, I see a strong and supple figure of medium height, and hear a smooth, rapid, uninterrupted voice, rather striking, almost without pauses, and at first without special emphasis.

The first sentences are usually general, the tone is a test one, the whole figure has not yet found its balance, the gestures are incomplete. The gaze is turned inward; the face is sullen and even vexed. His mind is seeking an approach to the audience. But all at once he reaches the kernel of the matter. The theme becomes clear. The speaker bends the upper part of his body, and sticks his middle finger in the edge of his vest. As a result of this double movement his head and hands stand out. The head in itself does not seem large on the small but sturdy body, well formed and rhythmical. But his brow and the bare, arched forehead are powerful. His arms are very active

186

but without exaggeration and nervousness. The hand is broad, short-fingered, "plebeian," strong. It has the same traits of virile good nature as the whole figure. One sees that best when the speaker is stirred on feeling an opponent's stratagem, or has successfully set a trap for him. Then Lenin's eyes look forth from their deep-set sockets. Even the indifferent listener is startled when he catches this look and waits to see what will happen. The edges of his cheek bones glow and soften in these moments of intense mental concentration, back of which one detects keen knowledge of people, relations, and situations. The lower part of the face with its reddish grey beard is almost in shadow. The voice loses its hardness, becomes flexible and soft, and in many moments astutely insinuating.

If there are adversaries in the audience, critical or hostile cries arise from time to time. In nine cases out of ten they are unanswered. The speaker says what he considers necessary, he speaks to those for whom what is said is necessary, and says it as he consider it necessary. Adroit readiness to fight does not suit his concentration. He only notices a hostile call in case this responds to the general course of his thoughts and helps him to come to the necessary conclusion more quickly. Then his answers are apt to be quite unexpected in their deadly simplicity. He reveals the situation unmercifully exactly where they had expected that he would veil it. The Mensheviki had that experience more than once in the early periods of the revolution when the accusations of the harm to democracy had all their freshness.

"Our newspapers are shut down."

"Naturally! But unfortunately not yet all. Soon they will be shut down entirely." (Stormy applause.) "The dictatorship of the proletariat will put a complete end to this disgraceful sale of bourgeois opium." (Stormy applause.)

The speaker draws himself up. Both hands are in his pockets. Here is not a trace of pose, the voice shows no rhetorical modulation, the whole figure, the position of his head with his lips pressed together, the cheek bones, and the slightly hoarse tones of his voice, express firm confidence in his justice and truth. "If you wish to strike, well, we will take good care of it."

When the speaker makes a joke, the lower part of his face projects more strongly, especially the mouth, which can laugh contagiously. The lines of his forehead and head grow softer, the eyes no longer glitter, but beam cheerfully, the strain of his bold mind is relieved by happiness and friendliness.

The leading feature in Lenin's speeches, as in his whole work, is his directness of purpose. What holds his speech together is not a formal plan, but a clear aim that pierces the consciousness of his listeners like a splinter.

And now the speech approaches its end. The separate points are established, the conclusions firmly drawn. The speaker looks like an exhausted workman who has finished his work. From time to time he passes his hand over his bald head with its drops of perspiration. His voice has sunk as a camp fire dies away. He is about to close. But one looks in vain for an ascending finale to crown the speech and without which ostensibly one cannot leave the platform. Others cannot, but Lenin can. There is no rhetorical winding up with him: he finishes the work and makes a point. "If we understand this, if we act thus, then we shall surely conquer" is a not unusual concluding sentence. Or: "One must strive for that, not in words, but in deeds." Or now and then more simple: "That is all that I wanted to say to you," nothing more. And this conclusion, which entirely corresponds to the nature of Lenin's eloquence and the nature of Lenin himself, by no means cools his audience. On the contrary, after just such a conclusion, "without effect," "pale," the listeners grasp once more, as if it were a single blaze of consciousness, all that Lenin had given them in his speech, and the audience breaks out into stormy, grateful, enthusiastic applause.

But Lenin has already gathered up his papers and quickly leaves the speaker's desk in order to escape the inevitable. His head drawn to his shoulders, his chin down, his eyes concealed by his brows, his mustache bristles angrily on the upper lip puckered in annoyance. The roaring handclapping grows, and hurls wave upon wave . . . "Long live . . . Lenin . . . Leader . . . Ilyich . . .".

1900s

LENIN'S METHOD OF WORK
by Nadezhda K. Krupskaya

NADEZHDA KONSTANTINOVA KRUPSKYA was Lenin's wife and lifelong companion. A member of the intelligentsia, she took an active part in the social-democratic movement from 1891 onwards. She and Lenin met soon after he came to St. Petersburg in 1894, and from then on they were always together. Nadezhda Konstantinova shared Lenin's exile both in Siberia and Europe and with him she played an important role in the underground movement. She also helped with the editing of *Iskra* (the spark), a revolutionary paper which appeared in Munich and was distributed by the underground in Russia. She also wrote books on her own of which *The Working Woman* and *Popular Education and Democracy* are the most important.

When Lenin returned to Russia from exile in 1917, Nadezhda Konstantinova accompanied her husband, participating actively in the preparations for the October Revolution. After the Revolution, she was given an important post in the education department of the new Soviet Government.

No matter what work Vladimir Ilyich undertook, he did it extremely thoroughly. He himself did a tremendous amount of the ordinary routine work. The more importance he attached to any particular work, the more would he delve into all the details.

189

At the end of the 'nineties, Vladimir Ilyich saw how difficult it was to establish in Russia an illegal newspaper, appearing regularly. On the other hand he attached tremendous organisational and agitational importance to an all-Russian newspaper that would elucidate from the Marxist standpoint all the events and facts of actual Russian life and the working-class movement that was beginning to develop more and more widely. He therefore selected a group of comrades, and decided to go abroad and organise the publication of such a newspaper there. *Iskra* was conceived by him and organised by him. Every number received exhaustive attention. Every word was thought out. And—what is a very characteristic detail—Vladimir Ilyich himself corrected the proofs of the whole paper. This was not because there was no one else to read the proofs (I quickly adapted myself to this work), but because he was anxious that no errors should slip in. First he read the proofs himself, then passed them to me, then looked over them again.

And it was the same with everything. He put in a great deal of work, studying and drawing up agrarian statistics. His notebooks contain a large number of carefully written-out tables. When he was dealing with figures that were of great importance, he even checked the additions, etc., of the printed tables. The careful verification of every fact and every figure was typical of Ilyich. He based his conclusions on fact.

Lenin did not rely on his memory, although he had an excellent one. He never cited facts from memory, "approximately," but always gave them with the greatest accuracy. He looked through piles of material (he read with extraordinary rapidity, just as he wrote), but whatever he wanted to remember he wrote down in his notebooks. Once when looking over my brochure, *Organisation of Self-Education,* he said I was wrong in stating that notes should only be made on the most necessary things—his experience had been otherwise. He used to read over his notes several times, which is evident from the various remarks, underlining, etc.

Sometimes, if the book were his own, he found it sufficient to make underlinings and marginal notes. On the cover he wrote the numbers of the pages marked, underlining them with one or several lines, according to the importance of the marked passages. He also re-read his own articles, making notes to them as well. Anything he noticed that led up to some new idea, he also underlined and noted the page on the cover. That was the way Ilyich organised his memory. He always remembered exactly what he had said, where, and in controversy with whom. In his books, speeches, and articles we find very few repetitions. It is true that over a period of years we encounter the same fundamental ideas in Ilyich's articles and speeches. This is because his utterances bear the imprint of a peculiar unity. But we do not find just an ordinary repetition of something already uttered. The same fundamental idea is advanced but as applied to new conditions, in a new concrete setting, and treating the question from a new aspect. I remember a talk with Ilyich when he had already fallen ill. We were talking about the volumes of his complete works that had just appeared. We spoke of how they reflected the experience of the Russian Revolution. We agreed that the volumes published should be utilised to illustrate how the basic, cardinal idea must inevitably be treated in varying ways, dependent on the changing concrete historical environment.

1916

THE NIGHT OF THE SIXTEENTH DECEMBER
by Prince Felix Youssoupoff

ONE OF THE strangest characters in the drama of the collapse of the Russian empire was Grigori Efimovich Rasputin, a Siberian peasant who called himself a holy man. Ignorant and debauched but endowed with a strange hypnotic power, Rasputin was taken up by a clique of St. Petersburg's highest society, who believed that he possessed a miraculous healing power. When the young Tsarevich, who suffered from hemophilia, was lying desperately ill in one of his recurrent crises, Rasputin was taken to the bedside of the sick child as a last resort. Whether by hypnosis or by some other means, he was able to stop the bleeding. Tsar Nicholas II and the Tsaritsa believed that Rasputin had saved their child's life and that he had been sent to them by God.

On more than one occasion Rasputin was able to repeat his miraculous cure, and soon his influence broadened until this ignorant, depraved peasant was advising his royal patrons on everything from cabinet posts to the conduct of the First World War.

In 1915, when the war was in a critical phase, the Tsar went to the front to take personal command of his army, leaving the affairs of the Russian empire to be administered by the Tsaritsa. Her only trusted adviser was Rasputin, whom she called "our friend."

It was an intolerable situation, and a group of young Russian aristocrats decided to put an end to it by liquidating Rasputin. They believed they were saving their country. While his fellow conspirators waited upstairs, Prince Felix Youssoupoff lured Rasputin into the dining room of his palace where the dramatic scene described in the pages that follow was enacted.

Time passed. I began to get impatient. I poured out two glasses, one for him [Rasputin], the other for myself. I placed his glass in front of him and began to drink out of my own, thinking that he would follow my example.

"Well, let me try it," said Rasputin, stretching out his hand for the wine. It was not poisoned.

Why I first gave him wine in an unpoisoned glass I am at a loss to explain.

He drank it with obvious pleasure. He became animated. "Now give me some Madeira," he said.

I got up to take another glass, but he protested. "Pour it into this one."

I had to give way.

By an apparent accident, however, I soon managed to knock his glass to the floor, where it smashed.

I took advantage of this to pour wine into one of the glasses containing cyanide of potassium.

He drank slowly, taking small sips at a time, just as if he had been a connoisseur.

His face did not change; but from time to time he put his hand to his throat as if he found slight difficulty in swallowing. He got up and moved about the room, and when I asked him whether anything was the matter, "Oh, nothing much," he said, "just an irritation in the throat."

There was a nerve-racking pause.

"That's very good Madeira. Give me some more."

The poison still had no effect.

I took no notice of the glass which he held out to me, but seized another poisoned one from the tray. I poured wine into it, and passed it to him.

He drained it: and still the poison had no effect.

There remained the third and last glass.

He looked at me with a cunning smile. I seemed to hear him say: "You see! you can't do me any harm."

But all of a sudden his expression changed into one of fiendish hatred.

I felt that he knew why I had brought him there, and what I intended to do to him. A mute and deadly conflict seemed to be taking place between us. A strange feeling of numbness took possession of me. My head reeled . . . I saw nothing . . . I do not know how long this lasted. . . .

I regained my presence of mind and offered him some tea.

While I was pouring out tea, he got up and paced the room. His eye fell on the guitar.

"Play something," he begged, "I love the way you sing."

He sat and listened attentively at first; but as I continued, his head dropped towards the table. He seemed half-asleep.

The moment I stopped he opened his eyes and looked at me with a calm and sad expression: "Sing another," he said.

Time passed . . . The hands of the clock pointed to half-past two. This nightmare had lasted over two hours.

Upstairs, too, patience had evidently become exhausted. The sounds from that quarter became pronounced, and I was afraid that my friends would come down.

"What's all that noise?" asked Rasputin.

"Probably it's the guests going away; I'll go and see."

As I entered the study [my friends] rushed towards me with revolvers in their hands. Questions showered on me.

"The poison has had no effect," I said.

"Impossible," exclaimed the Grand Duke. "The dose was amply sufficient."

With great difficulty I persuaded them to leave me to finish with Rasputin alone. They had qualms on my behalf.

But finally I took the Grand Duke's revolver and went down to the dining-room.

Rasputin was sitting at the table, just as I had left him. His head was sunken and he was breathing heavily.

"Are you feeling unwell?" I asked.

"Yes, my head is heavy and my stomach is burning. Give me another glass—that will ease me."

I poured him some Madeira; he drank it at a gulp and at once revived and regained his good spirits. All of a sudden he suggested that we should go to the gypsies. I refused on the ground that it was too late.

I had been watching every one of his movements in the expectation of a fatal issue; and now he was suggesting that we should go to the gypsies! But what amazed me most was that in spite of his instinctive knowledge and insight, he should now be so utterly unconscious of his approaching end.

How could his sharp eyes fail to observe that, clenched in my hand behind my back was a revolver?

As this thought flashed through my mind, I looked round for some reason or other, and my glance fell on a crystal crucifix. I rose and went up to it.

"What are you doing over there so long?" asked Rasputin.

"I love this cross; it's a very beautiful thing."

"Yes, it's a nice thing. How much did you pay for it?"

He came towards me.

"Grigori Efimovich, you had better look at the crucifix, and say a prayer before it."

Rasputin looked at me in amazement, and with a trace of fear.

I saw a new and unfamiliar expression in his eyes, a touch of gentleness and submission. He came right up to me, looking me full in the face, and he seemed to read in my glance something which he was not expecting. I realised that the supreme moment was at hand.

"God give me strength to end it all," I thought, and I slowly brought the revolver from behind my back. Rasputin was still standing motionless before me, his head turned to the right, and his eyes on the crucifix.

"Where shall I shoot?" I thought. "Through the temple or through the heart?"

A streak of lightning seemed to run through my body. I fired.

There was a roar as from a wild beast, and Rasputin fell heavily backwards on the bear-skin rug.

I heard a noise on the staircase: my friends were hurrying to my aid.

We examined the wound. The bullet had passed through the region of the heart. There could be no doubt about it; he was dead.

We all felt elated, so convinced were we that the events of the night would deliver Russia from ruin and dishonour.

1917

DAYS THAT ENDED THE RUSSIAN MONARCHY
by Alexander F. Kerensky

ALEXANDER FEODOROVICH KERENSKY first attracted attention as an eloquent defense lawyer for men who had been accused of revolutionary activities against the tsarist government. A member of the Socialist Revolutionary Party, Kerensky was elected to the Duma, the Russian parliament, in 1912, where he soon became the leader of the left-wing deputies.

In March 1917, when, in the face of mounting popular resentment against the continuance of a disastrous war, Tsar Nicholas II tried to dissolve the Duma, a great part of the army, backed by the workers, rose up in revolt. In the excerpt that follows, Kerensky gives an account of the uprising that resulted in the formation of a provisional government. He was its only socialist member and subsequently its premier.

On Monday, March 12, 1917, at about eight o'clock in the morning, I was awakened by a voice saying: "Get up! Nekrassof is on the telephone. He says the Duma has been dissolved, the Volinsk Regiment has mutinied and is leaving its barracks. You are wanted at the Duma at once."

The political situation had grown ominously stormy during the preceding days. It came to me with a jolt, but I soon perceived, or rather felt, that the decisive hour had struck.

I jumped up, dressed quickly and hurried to the Duma—a five minute walk.

At about half past eight I arrived at a small side entrance of the Tauride Palace, seat of the Duma, and here I was swept up by the whirlwind in which I was to live for eight months.

As I recall the events of that day—Russia standing at the parting of the ways—I feel again the tense anxiety which animated me then. As I approached the Duma, every step seemed to bring me closer to the quivering forces of newly awakened life, and when the aged doorkeeper, as usual, closed the door of the palace behind me I felt this time as if he were barring behind me forever the way back to the old Russia, the Russia that had still existed the day before and even in the early morning of that glorious, awe-inspiring Monday.

I ran down the long deserted corridor and at last found some deputies in the Catherine Hall. From them I learned that Rodzianko, President of the Duma, had received an order from Nicholas II dissolving the Duma at midnight on March twelfth; that he sent an urgent telegram to the Tsar at General Headquarters, and to the generals in command of the various fronts, saying that the revolt in Petrograd was spreading, that, in addition to the Volinsk Regiment, the Engineer Battalion of the Guards had mutinied, that the Preobrajensk Regiment was restive and was about to come out in the streets, etc.

Meanwhile developments in the city were gathering explosive momentum. One regiment after another had come out into the streets without officers. Some of the officers had been arrested and there were even isolated cases of murder. Everywhere the population was making common cause with the troops. Masses of workmen were pouring into the center of the city from the suburbs, and there was

197

lively firing in many quarters. Soon news was brought to us of skirmishing with the police. The government machine guns were firing on the people from roofs and belfries. The throng of soldiers and civilians in the streets gave no indication, however, of being moved by any clear aim or purpose. With each passing moment the deputies were becoming increasingly aware of the fact that the Duma was the only center of authority commanding respect and that it was essential to take a final, decisive, irrevocable step.

The anxiety and alarm concerning the populace gradually subsided and the deputies began to go more frequently to the windows of the palace, scanning the streets which now seemed to have taken on an air of portentious mystery.

"Where are your troops? Are they coming?" many of the deputies asked me. "My troops!" It had seemed in the last few days as if every one in the Duma had begun to look to me and to my closest associates as the center upon which the whole course of events depended.

The council of the party leaders met to consider the situation and to work out a plan of action to be submitted for approval to the unofficial meeting of the Duma. Those of us who met in the council laid aside all differences of party, class and age. We were dominated by one thing only: the realization that Russia was on the brink of ruin and that we must do our best to save her.

We, representatives of the opposition, now officially proposed what might be termed the revolutionary course. We demanded that the Duma go immediately into official session, taking no notice whatever of the order of dissolution. The majority did not agree with us. The council rejected our proposal, deciding that the Duma convene in unofficial session.

This refusal to continue in session formally was perhaps the greatest mistake of the Duma. It meant committing suicide at the very moment when its authority was supreme in the country and it might have played a decisive and fruitful part had it acted officially. The Duma died on the morning of March twelfth, the day when its strength and influence were at the highest.

Next day, March thirteenth, there were already two centers of authority: the Duma in unofficial session with its Temporary Committee, named as a provisional body to direct events, and the Council or Soviet of Workmen's and Soldiers' Deputies with its Executive Committee.

Some one called to me from the main entrance of the palace, saying, "The soldiers are coming!" I flew to a window to convince myself that it was actually so. I had no thought of what I would do next. From the window I saw soldiers, surrounded by a throng of civilians, lining up on the opposite side of the street. I gazed at them for a moment, and then, just as I was, in the black jacket which I wore during the entire Revolution, without hat or overcoat, I ran out through the main entrance to the soldiers for whom we had waited so long. I ran to the center gate that led from the garden into the street and welcomed the troops and the people in the name of the Duma and in my own behalf. They rushed towards me in confusion, surrounded me in a mass and listened.

Almost at the same moment deputies came up behind me at the palace gate. And then I addressed the troops and asked them to follow me into the Duma, to replace the guards and take over the defense of the building from the Tsarist troops.

After 3 P.M. the Duma was unrecognizable. The building was filled with civilians and troops, principally privates. From every direction people were coming to us for advice and instructions. The Temporary Committee of the Duma, which had just been established, was compelled immediately to assume the functions of executive authority. At midnight March thirteenth, there was no more wavering on the part of the Committee. It became for the time being the sovereign power of Russia.

1917

THE PEOPLE'S REVOLUTION
by John Reed

JOHN REED was an American writer and a Bolshevik sympathizer. In the excerpt that follows, he describes the November uprising that led to the overthrow of the liberal or moderate socialist provisional government under Kerensky. It was a defeat for democracy, and from that time on the Bolsheviks were in control of Russia. It was also a victory for the extreme left and, in time, for the Communist Party which, under Lenin, succeeded in dominating the Bolshevik government.

I returned to the Soviet Palace in Tsarskoye in the Regimental Staff automobile. Still the crowds of workers, soldiers and sailors pouring in and out, still the choking press of trucks, armoured cars, cannon before the door, and the shouting, the laughter of unwonted victory. Half a dozen red Guards forced their way through, a priest in the middle. This was Father Ivan, they said, who had blessed the Cossacks when they entered the town. I heard afterward that he was shot.

Dybenko [a member of the Committee for Military and Naval Affairs] was just coming out, giving rapid orders right and left. In his hand he carried a big revolver. An automobile stood with racing engine at the kerb. Alone, he climbed in the rear seat, and was off—off to Gatchina, to conquer Kerensky.

Toward nightfall he arrived at the outskirts of the town and went on afoot. What Dybenko told the Cossacks nobody knows, but the fact is that General Krasnov and his staff and several thousand Cossacks surrendered, and advised Kerensky to do the same.

As for Kerensky—I reprint here the deposition made by General Krasnov on the morning of November 14th:

"Gatchina, November 14th, 1917. To-day, about three o'clock (A.M.) I was summoned by the Supreme Commander (Kerensky). He was very agitated and very nervous.

" 'General,' he said to me, 'you have betrayed me. Your Cossacks declare categorically that they will arrest me and deliver me to the sailors.'

" 'Yes,' I answered, 'there is talk of it, and I know that you have no sympathy anywhere.'

" 'But the officers say the same thing.'

" 'Yes, most of all it is the officers who are discontented with you.'

" 'What shall I do? I ought to commit suicide!'

" 'If you are an honorable man, you will go immediately to Petrograd with a white flag, you will present yourself to the Military Revolutionary Committee, and enter into negotiations as Chief of the Provisional Government.'

" 'All right. I will do that, General.'

" 'I will give you a guard, and ask that a sailor go with you.'

" 'I'll leave to-night!'

" 'Why? That would be a flight. Leave calmly and openly, so that every one can see that you are not running away.'

" 'Very well. But you must give me a guard on which I can count.'

" 'Good.'

"I went out and called the Cossack Russkov, of the Tenth Regiment of the Don, and ordered him to pick out ten Cossacks to accompany the Supreme Commander. Half an hour later the Cossacks came to tell me that Kerensky was not in his quarters, that he had run away.

"I gave the alarm and ordered that he be searched for, supposing that he could not have left Gatchina, but he could not be found."

And so Kerensky fled, alone, "disguised in the uniform of a sailor," and by that act lost whatever popularity he had retained among the Russian masses.

I went back to Petrograd riding on the front seat of an auto truck, driven by a workman and filled with Red Guards. We had no kerosene, so our lights were not burning. The road was covered with the proletarian army going home, and new reserves pouring out to take their places. Immense trucks, like ours, columns of artillery, wagons, loomed up in the night, without lights, as we were. We hurtled furiously on, wrenched right and left to avoid collisions that seemed inevitable, scraping wheels, followed by the epithets of pedestrians.

Across the horizon spread the glittering lights of the capital, immeasurably more splendid by night than by day, like a dike of jewels heaped on the barren plain.

The old workman who drove held the wheel in one hand, while with the other he swept the far-gleaming capital in an exultant gesture.

"Mine!" he cried, his face all alight. "All mine now! My Petrograd!"

Bibliography

The extracts included in this book may be found in the following sources:

Page 1. *The History of Herodotus,* translated by George Rawlinson. New York: Dial Press, Inc., 1928.

Page 5. *The Fasti, Tristia and Pontic Epistles,* by Ovid. Translated by Henry T. Riley. London: George Bell & Sons, Ltd., 1903.

Page 8. *The Russian Primary Chronicle,* by Vladimir Monomakh. Translated by Samuel Cross. Cambridge: Harvard University Press, 1930.

Page 10. *A General History and Collection of Voyages and Travels,* edited by Robert Kerr. Edinburgh: William Blackwood, 1811–16.

Page 12. *Of Divers Particular Things,* by Sigmund von Herberstein. In Eden: *Decades.* London, 1555.

Page 15. *Le Stoglav,* edited by Eduard Champion. Paris: Librairie Ancienne Honoré Champion, 1920.

Page 19. *The Discovery of Muscovy.* From the collection of Richard Hakluyt. London: Cassell & Co. Ltd., 1904.

Page 21. *Of the Russe Common Wealth,* by Giles Fletcher. London: Printed by T. D. for Thomas Chaude, 1951.

Page 24. *Anthology of Russian Literature,* by Leo Wiener. New York: G. P. Putnam's Sons, 1902.

Page 28. *A Revelation Concerning the Particulars of the Rebellion Lately Raised in Muscovy by Stenko Razin.* Printed by Theo. Newcomb, 1672.

Page 33. *Travels into Divers Parts of Europe and Asia,* by Father Avril, S.J. London: Printed by Tim Goodwin, 1693.

Page 37. *Travels into Muscovy, Persia and Part of the East Indies,* by Cornelis de Bruyn. Translated from the French. London: Printed for A. Bettesworth & C. Hitch, 1737.

Page 42. *The State of Russia Under the Present Czar,* by Captain John Perry. London: B. Tooke, 1716.

Page 45. *An Account of Russia in the Year 1710,* by Charles Lord Witworth. Printed at Strawberry Hill, 1743.

Page 47. *Memoirs of the Princess Daschkaw.* London: Henry Colburn, 1840.

Page 52. *Seven Britons in Imperial Russia,* edited by Peter Putnam. Princeton: Princeton University Press, 1952.

Page 54. *New Voyages and Travels.* London: Printed for Sir Richard Phillips & Co., 1822. (From *Adventures of Michaelow, a Russian Captive,* Written by Himself, 1771.)

Page 59. *Secret Memoirs of the Court of Petersburg,* translated by Charles François Masson. London: Longman & Rees, 1800.

Page 62. *A Journey Through the Crimea to Constantinople. Letters from the Right Honorable Elizabeth, Lady Craven to His Serene Highness the Margrave of Brandenburg, Anspach and Bareith.* London & Dublin: Printed for G. S. S. & J. Robinson, 1789.

Pages 69 and 73. *Philosophical, Political and Literary Travels in Russia During the Years 1788 & 1789,* by Chantreau. Perth: R. Morrison & Son and London: Vernor & Hood, 1794.

Pages 77 and 80. *The Most Remarkable Years in the Life of Augustus von Kotzebue,* by Himself. London: Printed for Richard Phillips, 1802.

Page 83. *The Russian Journals of Martha and Catherine Wilmot,* edited by the Marchioness of Londonderry and H. M. Hyde. London: Macmillan & Co. Ltd., 1934.

Page 88. *The Memoirs of Count Paul Christophorovich Grabbé.* Moscow, 1873.

Page 92. *With Napoleon in Russia, the Memoirs of General de Caulaincourt, Duke of Vicenza.* New York: William Morrow & Co., Inc., 1935.

Page 95. *The Corsican. A Diary of Napoleon's Life in his Own Words.* Boston: Houghton Mifflin Co., 1910.

Page 97. *Memoirs of John Quincy Adams,* edited by Charles Francis Adams. Phladelphia: J. B. Lippincott Co., 1874.

Page 102. *Diary of George Mifflin Dallas.* Philadelphia: J. B. Lippincott Co., 1892.

Page 106. *Childhood, Boyhood, Youth,* by Lyof N. Tolstoi. New York: Thomas Y. Crowell Co., 1886.

Page 109. *Revelations of Russia,* by Charles Frederick Henningsen. London: Henry Colburn, 1844.

Pages 113 and 138. *Tourgueneff and his French Circle,* edited by E. Halperine-Kaminsky. Translated by Ethel M. Arnold. New York: Henry Holt and Company, 1898.

Page 116. *The Crimea in 1854 and 1894,* by General Sir Evelyn Wood. London: Chapman & Hall Ltd., 1895.

Page 119. *Adventures in Czarist Russia,* by Alexandre Dumas. Translated by A. E. Murch. London: Peter Owen Ltd., 1960.

Page 123. *Sketches of Russian Life,* by an Anonymous English-man. London: Chapman & Hall Ltd., 1866.

Pages 127 and 163. *Russia,* by Theophile Gautier. Philadelphia: John C. Winston Co., 1905.

Page 130. *The Innocents Abroad,* by Mark Twain. New York: Harper & Bros., 1905.

Page 133. *Memoirs of a Revolutionist,* by P. Kropotkin. Boston: Houghton Mifflin Co., 1899.

Page 140. *Sixteen Years in Siberia. Some Experiences of a Russian Revolutionary,* by Leo Deutsch. New York: E. P. Dutton & Co., Inc., 1903.

Page 144. *My Russian and Turkish Journals,* by the Dowager Marchioness of Dufferin and Ava. New York: Charles Scribner's Sons, 1916.

Page 148. *The Court of Alexander III, Letters of Mrs. Lothrop.* Philadelphia: John C. Winston Co., 1910.

Page 151. *Siberia and the Exile System,* by George Kennan. New York: Century Co., 1891.

Page 155. *In the Land of Tolstoy,* by Jonas Stadling and Will Reason. New York: Thomas Whittaker, 1897.

Page 160. *Fragments From My Diary, by Maxim Gorky.* New York: Robert McBride & Co., 1924.

Page 167. *Count Tolstoy on the War Between Russia and Japan.* New York: Frederick A. Stokes Co., 1904.

Page 172. *Dawn in Russia,* by Henry W. Nevinson, New York: Harper & Bros., 1906.

Page 176. *A Year in Russia,* by Maurice Baring. New York: E. P. Dutton & Co., Inc., 1907.

Page 179. *Through Savage Europe,* by Harry de Windt. Philadelphia: J. B. Lippincott Co., 1907.

Page 182. *Undiscovered Russia,* by Stephen Graham. London: Bodley Head Ltd., 1913.

Page 186. *Lenin,* by Leon Trotsky. New York: Minton, Balch & Co., 1925.

Page 189. *Memories of Lenin,* by Nadezhda K. Krupskaya. Translated by Eric Verney. New York: International Publishers Co., Inc., 1930.

Page 192. *Rasputin,* by Prince Felix Youssoupoff. New York: Dial Press, Inc., 1927.

Page 196. *The Catastrophe,* by Alexander F. Kerensky. New York: Appleton-Century, 1927.

Page 200. *Ten Days that Shook the World,* by John Reed. New York: Boni & Liveright, 1919.